Melville Dissertations, 1924–1980

Melville Dissertations, 1924-1980

1924-1980

AN ANNOTATED BIBLIOGRAPHY
AND SUBJECT INDEX

John Bryant
With the Sponsorship of the Melville Society

Greenwood Press
Westport, Connecticut • London, England

Library of Congress Cataloging in Publication Data

Bryant, John.
  Melville dissertations, 1924-1980.

  Bibliography: p.
  Includes indexes.
  1. Melville, Herman, 1819-1891—Bibliography.
2. Dissertations, Academic—Bibliography.   I. Title.
Z8562.58.B79   1983   016.813'3   83-5683
[PS2386]
ISBN 0-313-23811-1 (lib. bdg.)

Library of Congress Catalog Card Number: 83-5683
ISBN: 0-313-23811-1

First published in 1983

Greenwood Press
A division of Congressional Information Service, Inc.
88 Post Road West, Westport, Connecticut 06881

Printed in the United States of America

10 9 8 7 6 5 4 3 2 1

IN MEMORY
of
John Francis Bryant

(1921-1981)

Scientist and Artist

Contents

Acknowledgments

My work could not have begun without the foundations provided in previous editions by Tyrus Hillway, Hershel Parker, Joel Myerson, and Arthur H. Miller, Jr. In particular, Arthur Miller has provided many lists, a few notes, and patient advice, and made the transition from compiler to compiler effortless.

I would like to thank the administration and staff of the Newberry Library for their financial assistance and congeniality during my summer there in 1981. Richard Colles Johnson, curator of the Melville Collection, was indispensible in giving advice and procuring texts. I would also like to thank the Department of English, the College of Liberal Arts, and the Shenango Valley Campus of the Pennsylvania State University for their encouragement and financial assistance in this project.

From time to time certain individuals were helpful in procuring titles. Warner Berthoff kindly double-checked Harvard's files for possible errant theses, and Jeanne Templeton and Larry L. Greenfield of the University of Chicago also provided several otherwise unlisted titles.

Hennig Cohen and Donald Yannella (past and present Secretaries of the Melville Society) were kind enough to invite me to join the project. Mr. Yannella has given sage counsel and energetic support at crucial times. Mr. Cohen has been inspirational in matters that go far deeper than sub-sub-bibliography. I am grateful to them, and thank them for their consultations, consolations, and friendship.

Finally, I wish to thank Virginia Blanford; gladly did she file (once) and gladly teach.

Introduction

This bibliography provides scholars with a record of completed doctoral theses devoted entirely or in part to the life and works of Herman Melville. It is both a testament to the author's stature and a guide for present and future Melvilleans. Filed, numbered, annotated, and indexed herein are 531 dissertations composed over the past fifty years. No other American writer of the nineteenth or twentieth centuries (with the possible exception of Hawthorne) has inspired as many works. The sheer bulk of these neatly bound typescripts attests to Melville's continued, indeed growing, reputation, and this fact alone would justify a bibliography such as this. But if the dissertation is, for the most part, little more than a scholar's juvenilia, a compilation of Melville dissertations is indeed a paltry monument to a great writer. For Melville, who would have winced over all this fuss and "heady" speculation, it would be a deliciously ironic monument as well. He knew well that so much theory could not outweigh the "plump sphericity" of his fictions.

The author might smile, too, over the added irony that this labor of a Pale Usher before you should serve as a doctoral candidate's guide. In his work, Melville repeatedly deprecates the guidebook; it is physically dated and metaphysically absurd. Experience is our only guide. We who have witnessed the expansion of graduate schools over the past decades of New Criticism, in which one "reading" begets another, might add to Melville's doubts one of our own: not only are guidebooks misleading but the streets this particular book leads us through seem suspiciously insignificant. In former days when topics outnumbered graduate students and a Hayford, Bezanson, Horsford, or Foster could write a reasonably definitive dissertation, the doctoral thesis was generally expected to make a unique contribution. Today, however, the wholesale abandonment of this principle seems apparent in the sizable degree of duplication of thesis topics evident in these pages. And yet it is outrageous to assume that today's many dissertations are repetitious, insignificant, or without merit.

In an age of relativism, a "definitive" interpretation of a literary work is a contradiction in terms. Interpretation is an ongoing process of debate, and each interpretive dissertation is an exercise in approach, the expression of a single voice rising out of heated discussion. Melville's durability in the graduate schools is due in part to the fact that his works have become the touchstones of innumerable and timely debates ranging from politics and race to aesthetics and film. None, then, can reasonably expect to find *the* meaning of Melville in any of these dissertations. In each, though, we hope for something more than a hollow drum sounding off in a language come to be known as "dissertationese." We expect the student of Melville to resurrect an old debate, put one to rest, or even create a new one, and to do this with insight and sensitivity. In reading these theses I have gladly found more insight than error (although errors surely exist), more felicity of style than turgidity.

Finally, if we are to offer any happy adjective for a Melville dissertation, it would not be that it is "definitive" (for this suggests preconceived assumptions on the reviewer's behalf) or "unique" (for this suggests idiosyncracy for its own sake), but that it is "useful." A dissertation is good if it can be of use to others in achieving further insight. In light of this, the subject index prepared for this edition of *Melville Dissertations* is designed to lead present scholars to what might be useful to them. It will also indicate to future scholars the "state of debate" in their chosen topic. It is hoped that a timely scrutiny of this volume will prevent the stillborn creation of "yet another reading" of Melville.

This annotated bibliography is the product of several souls laboring at various times over the past three decades. In 1953, Tyrus Hillway compiled *Doctoral Dissertations on Herman Meville.* Nine years later he collaborated with Hershel Parker to produce the *Directory of Melville Dissertations* (1962). Under the aegis of the Melville Society, Joel Myerson and Arthur H. Miller, Jr., brought the bibliography up to date for 1971 with the publication of *Melville Dissertations: An Annotated Directory* (1972). Their plan was to annotate as many dissertations as possible and to provide yearly supplements in *Melville Society Extracts.* Mr. Miller bravely performed this task for two years, at the end of which time he found something better to do. The present author was called upon to take over in 1978. Young and unwise, I proposed to consolidate the *Directory* and its supplements, annotate theses from 1971 to the present (which involved reading 280 works, a number that more than doubled the total Melville dissertations), edit past annotations, create subject and author indices, and say a few words about trends in Melville dissertations. Having bravely performed these tasks, I now hope (like my predecessors) to find something better to do.

The following pages will review the procedure in creating the bibliography, outline its format, and briefly assess the nature of its contents.

I

Retrieving Melville dissertation titles from *Dissertation Abstracts International (DAI)* and the *MLA Bibliography* is relatively easy with the aid of a computer. But not all universities submit to *DAI* (Harvard and Chicago, in particular) and not all theses include Melvill's name in the title or use it as a "descriptor" for the computer. Hence, some titles do not appear in print-outs. Double-checking the *Cumulative Dissertation Index* under categories likely to include Melville has yielded a few items which might otherwise have been lost. Foreign dissertations present more obvious problems, but several overseas titles havè been found in such resources as *Dissertations in English and American Literature* and *English and American Studies in German.*

In annotating each of the 1970s theses, I have tried to record rather than criticize the approach, theories, applications, and texts used by each author. To achieve some degree of uniformity in this respect and in style, I have sidestepped author-composed abstracts (which can be maddeningly uninformative at times) and gone directly to the thesis itself. (The Newberry Library maintains a thorough collection of Melville dissertations.) In those rare instances in which the thesis was unavailable for direct inspection, I resorted to editing the author's abstract as published in *DAI.* Very few entries have escaped some form of annotation. As stated earlier, the annotations are content reports, not critiques. If a writer proposes that Moby Dick is really Melville's wife, I report that argument without critical asides. It is, I feel, the reader's job to determine the usefulness and ultimate value of the works listed here. To be sure, the five or so sentences provided for each thesis cannot do justice to the entire content of the work itself. It is not likely that everyone will be totally satisfied with the summary I have created for his or her thesis. For this I apologize, but in all cases I have tried to adopt the author's perspective and critical vocabulary in order to present each work in its most favorable light. Furthermore, recognizing that quotations out of context can make a writer appear foolish, I have quoted sparingly and only with the hope of achieving clarity. In all, the reader will readily understand that these annotations can give only a limited insight into the work itself.

In editing annotations of pre-1970 dissertations, I have generally expanded fragments into sentences and removed unnecessary grammatical structures and language.

The formats for entry and annotation are as follows. Each entry is listed by year of completion and alphabetically within each year. Each consists of an author, full title, school, year of completion, page length, and (if available) a University Microfilm order number. Unless otherwise indicated, dissertations are written in the language in which the title appears. If the thesis is listed in a source other than *DAI* or the *MLA Bibliography*, the source is indicated at the end of the entry. Finally, each entry is numbered for easy reference.

At the end of any given annotation, the reader is likely to find a curious selection of abbreviations, numbers, and article or book citations. For those theses that devote only partial attention to Melville, I have used "HM:" to indicate page references to Melville sections. When available, *Dissertation Abstracts* numbers (prefixed "DA:") or *English and American Studies in German* listings (EASG) appear parenthetically after the annotation so that interested readers can search out the author's abstract before ordering microfilms or copies of the complete thesis. If the annotation is derived from an author's abstract, this, too, will be indicated parenthetically at the end. Finally, articles and books derived from or related to dissertations are listed as supplements to the annotations following the prefix "See:."

Following the entries are author, school, and subject indices. In each case the index numbers refer to entries, not pages. Only the subject index requires further discussion. In compiling it I drew headings directly from dissertation titles and the annotations. Included here are authors and texts treated in conjunction with Melville, texts from the Melville canon, and themes, philosophies, genres, imagery, characters, and techniques explored in the theses. I have not attempted to index the critical approaches adopted by the writers. I have also added logical cross-reference categories (such as biography, politics, or character type) to help the reader pull related topics together. Obviously, the index is only as thorough as the titles are descriptive and the annotations are complete. It should not be taken as a comprehensive index to the content of all dissertations on Melville, but rather to this listing of those dissertations.

II

A significant by-product of this bibliography is that it is a virtual storehouse of data on the volume and shape of the Melville "industry." As suggested earlier, Melville scholarship has generally outstripped production in fields devoted to other equally important American writers including Poe, Emerson, Whitman, James, Twain, and Faulkner. In this respect (for good or ill) Melville is for Americanists, on a modest scale, what Shakespeare and his mighty industry are for Britainists; and, accordingly, the works referred to here might serve as a representative sample of the rapid growth and varying trends in various humanistic fields in the universities over the past fifty years.

Since 1924, the number of Melville dissertations has doubled for each decade. But in the 1970s, production more than doubled the total number of theses that had accumulated over the previous four decades. The 291 dissertations written at that time sent the total figure up to 531. The number of institutions producing Melville dissertations has also grown (but at a slightly reduced yearly rate) from seventeen schools in the early decades (1920s, 1930s, and 1940s) to 108 in the 1970s.

Over the years, Yale has produced far more theses (twenty-nine) than any other single university. But this figure does not communicate the full impact of Yale's contribution, for that school's first Melvilleans of the 1940s (Sealts, Foster, Bezanson, Hayford, Hillway, Davis, Gilman, Wright, Feidelson, and others have in turn directed numerous dissertations on Melville at various separate institutions. Therefore, while Yale's own Melville production lagged in the 1950s and 1960s, Yale Ph.D's (at Wisconsin and Northwestern, in particular) were busy creating a sizable second generation of Melvilleans. In the 1970s "newcomers" to the list of top producers included Indiana, Duke, SUNY-Buffalo, Ohio State, and Penn. Overall, the top ten producers of Melville dissertations are Yale (twenty-nine), Indiana (seventeen), Wisconsin (seventeen), Duke (fifteen), Northwestern (fifteen), Chicago (thirteen), Columbia (thirteen), Minnesota (thirteen), New York University (twelve), and SUNY-Buffalo (twelve).

In comparing Melville with other writers and thinkers, graduate students up through the 1960s found affinities with the following individuals: Horace Bushnell, Byron, Camus, Carlyle, Chateaubriand, Coleridge, Conrad, Cooper, Dickens, Dostoevsky, George Eliot, Emerson, Faulkner, Glasgow, Hawthorne, Irving, James, Kierkegaard, Malcolm Lowry, Milton, Theodore Parker, Poe, Shakespeare, Thoreau, Tourgée, Lionel Trilling, and Herman Wouk. A similar list of influential "ancients," contemporaries, and moderns reveals some repetition in the 1970s and yet a good deal of new exploration. The relationships between Melville and Byron, Camus, Carlyle, Conrad, Cooper, Emerson, Hawthorne, Kierkegaard, Poe, and Twain seem to hold a constant spell over Melvilleans, as well they should. The Hawthorne connection remains the dominant concern. He appears in eleven works. Newer (and perhaps bolder) connections have been studied (or created) in works focusing on such predecessors as Cervantes, Spenser, Shaftesbury, and Sterne. Duyckinck appears in two theses, as does Matthew Arnold. Melville's relationship to the arts is treated in works on Cole, Allston, and Wagner. His connection to modern writers has grown in interesting directions: the author appears beside Ellison, Mailer, Pynchon, Ken Kesey, Robert Lowell, Charles Olson, and Robert Creeley. One predictably recondite thesis compares Melville and Wittgenstein.

III

An examination of the topics and approaches taken in these works will yield a more precise assessment of the trends in Melville dissertations. My conclusions here, I believe, are "eminently safe." No single critical trend has dominated more than a fraction of the output especially in the more recent decades, but certain movements are clearly discernible. Some Melvilleans have continued debates (was Melville a democrat or monarchist; is *Billy Budd* an affirmation; how many confidence men can dance on the bow of the *Fidèle*?); some have applied new theories to basic texts (rhetorical criticism, phenomenology, semiotics and structuralism); some propose a negative, others a positive construction of Melville's life and works; some search out image patterns, metaphors, and participles; some have reinvented the wheel of ambiguity and reality. Relatively few, I would say, have created works that may be considered useful reference *tools* which might enhance our perception of a text (as text) or expand our understanding of the social and intellectual influences on the author's thought and art.

1924-1950

The earliest treatments of Melville emphasize the author's early life, thought, and sea narratives. Generally speaking, biography, textual matters, and influence studies outweigh thematic or purely interpretive works. The 1930s, for instance, gave us Hetherington's study of reviews (see entry 4), Braswell on Christianity (5), Anderson on the South Seas (7), and Mansfield on New York (9). With the 1940s came the Yale School which laid important groundwork for future study. Foster's edition of *CM* (14) and Bezanson's of *Clarel* (19), Sealts's work on Melville's reading (18) and Wright's on the Bible (34), Hayford's examination of the Hawthorne connection (24) and Feidelson's on symbolism (30) remain landmarks in the field. Equally important are Gilman's and Davis's treatments of *M* (28) and *R* (29), respectively. Finally, a few theses, such as Hillway's on nineteenth century science (21) and Oliver's on progress (13), treat Melville's intellectual and social milieu.

1951-1960

To a certain degree, interest in Melville made its most dramatic leap in the 1950s. The author no longer resided solely at Yale. Indeed, the number of schools producing work on Melville more than doubled. (This is the highest rate of increase in schools for the fifty-year period.) Furthermore, because New Criticism was in full swing and Melville was well suited for the eyes of close readers, the decade witnessed an influx of interpretive theses. To be sure, biography, textual matters, and influences were not abandoned. The decade produced a study of Melville's borrowings from seventeenth century writers (88), his orientation to the Near East (76), his whaling years (46), his magazine contributions (91), and critical editions of the journals (42) and the poems (92). Melville's receptions in France (62), Germany (83, 87), and the Soviet Union (54) were recorded, and one thesis focused exclusively on the Melville Revival during this century (43). But the bulk of the 1950s essays were interpretive. Still useful today are Rosenberry's study of the comic spirit (56), Stern's of theme and craft (68), and Bowen's of self and experience (73). A smattering of theses continued the debates on evil, tragic vision, nihilism, and time. One examined color imagery, and a few took on narrative problems. Melville's applicability to social issues, and in particular race, were demonstrated in two theses, including Kaplan's work on America's "national sin" (86).

1961-1970

The 1960s was an expansive age, even for Melville. The number of completed dissertations represented an increase of 256 percent over the previous decade. Equally expansive was the range of topics that graduate students drew upon: sports, witchcraft and demonology, seamen, survivors, loneliness, communication, failure, chaos, order, evolution, and the visual arts, among others. Several works focused on mythology, including Franklin's study of Hindu myth (96). From a philosophical perspective, Melville was seen as a transcendentalist and existentialist, a skeptic and a prophet. Dissertations examining social issues and Melville's life include two works on race, Parker's study of Melville's political milieu (120), and Charters on the Berkshires (133). Another biographical contribution is a study of Elizabeth Shaw and her not-always-enviable marriage to the author (211). A useful biographical tool is Cowen's massive compilation of Melville's marginalia (134).

Amidst the varied topics of the 1960s, certain trends can be discerned. Perhaps the most significant was the shift to rhetorical criticism, narrative, and point of view. Eleven theses focused on Melville's narrators; four on the structure of his novels; two on romance. Two important works dealing with such aesthetic matters are Seelye's study of irony (102) and Barbour's on the composition of *MD* (222). Genre studies also expanded in this period and brought us works on the grotesque, the burlesque, the gothic, the anatomy, the family novel, and the military novel. Melville's aesthetics, prose theory, and poetics were discussed in individual theses as well. Finally, three dissertations focused on the transformation of Melville's fiction into other genres, principally drama, opera, and film.

Running parallel to the interest in fictive structures is the shift in the 1960s toward Melville's later works. Contributing to this trend are Branch's edition of *CM* (223), Bickley's study of the short fiction (190), Dryden's on form (135), two works on the late fiction as a whole, three on *Clarel*, two on the shorter poems, two on *IP*, one on *P*, and three examining aspects of the confidence game, ranging from Bergmann's source study (189) to Wadlington's rhetorical analysis (170). Finally, a third trend that would give impetus and direction to the study of imagery in the latter half of the decade and on into the next was the phenomenological approach adopted by Brodtkorb in his treatment of Ishmael and Melville's symbology (113).

1971-1980

The 1970s have given us, by far, the most Melville dissertations, so many that they are best treated in four rough categories that deal with: 1) Aesthetics and romanticism, 2) Genre, structure, and character, 3) Themes and imagery, and 4) Language.

Relatively few theses took on problems in the area of Melville's aesthetic theory and relationship to other arts; much remains to be explored. Two works deal with specific artists known to Melville, and individual studies examine Melville's treatment of the artist (407), his "theatricality" (427), and his debt to Goethe, Schiller, and Arnold (472). A major focus is on the picturesque, the sublime, and landscape (six theses). Romantic theory is the issue in four other works. One thesis also takes on Shelley (281), and four discuss problems of American romanticism (savagery, wilderness, and nature.)

The 1970s saw a resurgence of interest in two genres, comedy and allegory. Picking up where Rosenberry left off are nine dissertations dealing with Melville's comic spirit, including Wakefield on Shaftesbury (337), Bryant on geniality in the later fiction (375), Mushabac on humor (456), two theses on the grotesque, three on the confidence man, and one on the Yankee peddler. In addition are Wilmes on satire (435), and two works on parody. Melvilleans responded to important redefinitions of allegory established in the 1960s with four theses on that topic, two on symbolism, and one on the Puritan parable (501). Also of interest was Melville's use of picaresque (three works) and of Cervantes's quixotic style (two works). While the short fiction is a growing concern these days, only three theses examined Melville's use of the tale as a genre. Finally, one thesis is devoted to Melville's "mannerist" novels (517) and one to film (299).

A significant proportion of the dissertations dealt with structural matters (for example, 268) and narrative voice (8 works). Three take on Melville's rhetorical strategies. Others explore such narrative devices as the dream (452), documents (443), and *leitmotif* (525). Two treat "open form." Several theses examine characters (for example, 332); two deal with masks.

Works treating Melville's themes can be subdivided (again roughly) into those principally 1) theological or philosophical, 2) sociological, and 3) psychological. A fourth category encompasses imagery.

Whether Melville had faith or not is a debate carried on in at least five dissertations (including Milder, 287). Of equal interest during the decade was Melville's apocalyptic and prophetic use of fiction (six works). Three theses, including one on perfectionism (353), treat antinomianism. Four take on the problems of evil and determinism, and one discusses Manicheism (338). Finally, one focuses on "Plinlimmon's theme" (444).

The dominant sociological theme concerned Melville's perspective on race (ten dissertations, including two on Indians). Melville's treatments of women, and of men in relation to women, are discussed in four works. And one thesis (363) attempts to tie racist and sexist views together. Melville's political theory and evolving conceptions of democracy are explored in five works. Other studies examine Melville's portrayal of the white collar worker (516), his attitude toward Wall Street (296), and his awareness of American law and judicial procedure (397).

Melville and psychology have always gone hand in hand. Students continued in the 1970s to exploit the kinship. We find two or three theses devoted to each of the following psychic phases of life as they are manifested in Melville's works: innocence, initiation, loneliness, madness, and the creative process. Five works take a strictly psychoanalytic approach. Others explore family structure (485), Pierre's homosexuality (502), and transcendental meditation (326).

The phenomenological approach introduced by J. Hillis Miller and applied to Melville by Paul Brodtkorb has shaped much of the decade's studies of imagery. Two dissertations have been written on each of three image patterns: the body, the home, and time and the circle. Additional works have focused on Melville's domestic architecture; his use of vast dimensions, heights, and volumes; of eating, drinking, and smoking; of navigation; reflections; and walls. In a more traditional vein, two works have examined Melville's allusions to classical mythology, and one focuses on his borrowings from almanacs.

Finally, a number of dissertations have scrutinized Melville's use of language. Useful tools for the scholar are computer assisted concordances of *Moby-Dick* (440), *Clarel* (487), and *Billy Budd* (505). Also of interest are a list of metaphors throughout the fiction (521) and a dictionary of Melville's sea vocabulary (474). Works focusing on Wittgenstein, semiotics, Melville's stylistic debt to Carlyle, and his use of synonyms and repetitions take a more interpretive stance.

In his lucid and readable work of scholarship, *The Trying-out of Moby-Dick*, Howard P. Vincent drew the following trope:

> If a whaleship was Melville's "Yale College and my Harvard," one should bring the record up to date and say that the whaling books (his fish documents) were then his graduate school, and *Moby-Dick* the doctoral dissertation—which itself a hundred years later would provoke dissertations. (p. 102)

In 1949, when these words were written, Melville's "whale" had "provoked" only thirty-four doctoral dissertations. Professor Vincent had no way of telling then that in thirty years this figure would amount to only 6 percent of the total dissertation output. The Melville industry at the graduate level has been, over the years, robust; some might say too robust. What mark the most recent theses will make is impossible to tell. Future trends are equally impossible to predict. No doubt production in the 1980s will reflect the decreasing enrollments in our graduate schools. Some hint of a decline can also be seen in the fact that yearly output in the 1970s decreased from a high of forty-one dissertations in 1972 to a low of twenty in 1978. Whatever the figures bear out, Melville's position as a focal point in American art and life remains secure.

List of Abbreviations

BB	*Billy Budd*
BP	*Battle-Pieces*
CM	*The Confidence-Man*
DA	*Dissertation Abstracts International (Dissertation Abstracts,* prior to volume 30)
DEAL	*Dissertations in English and American Literature*
EASG	*English and American Studies in German*
HM	Herman Melville
IP	*Israel Potter*
M	*Mardi*
MD	*Moby-Dick*
Mosses	"Hawthorne and His Mosses"
O	*Omoo*
P	*Pierre*
PT	*Piazza Tales*
R	*Redburn*
T	*Typee*
WJ	*White-Jacket*

Bibliographic Entries

1924-1950

1924

1. Ross, Ernest C. <u>The Development of the English Sea Novel</u>. University of Virginia, 1924.

   See: Ross, Ernest C. <u>The Development of the English Sea Novel from DeFoe to Conrad</u>. Ann Arbor, Mi.: Edwards Brothers, 1926 [Mimeographed].

2. Starr, Nathan Comfort. <u>The Sea in the English Novel from DeFoe to Melville</u>. Harvard University, 1928.

   Melville's sea novels are related to others of the time. HM: 315-62.

1932

3. Hurley, Leonard Burwell. <u>The American Novel, 1830-1850: Its Reflection of Contemporary Religious Conditions, with a Bibliography of Fiction</u>. University of North Carolina at Chapel Hill, 1932.

   The focus is on the south sea novels and Melville's comments on missionaries. Bibliography is now superseded. HM: 302-10, 770-84.

1933

4. Hetherington, Hugh W. <u>The Reputation of Herman Melville in America</u>. University of Michigan, 1933.

   See: Hetherington, Hugh W. <u>Melville's Reviewers, British and American: 1846-1891</u>. Chapel Hill, N.C.: University of North Carolina Press, 1961.

1934

5. Braswell, William. Herman Melville and Christianity. University of
Chicago, 1934.

> See: Braswell, William. Melville's Religious Thought. Durham,
> N.C.: Duke University Press, 1943; rpt. New York: Pageant Books,
> 1959.

6. White, Viola Chittenden. Symbolism in Herman Melville's Writings.
University of North Carolina at Chapel Hill, 1934. 391 pages.

> Although Melville's symbolism expresses phases in his religious
> thought, the ideas thus expressed are actually romantic.

1935

7. Anderson, Charles Roberts. With Melville in the South Seas.
Columbia University, 1935.

> See: Anderson, Charles Roberts. Melville in the South Seas. New
> York: Columbia University Press, 1939; rpt. New York: Dover
> Publications, 1966. Journal of a Cruise to the Pacific Ocean,
> 1842-1844, in the Frigate United States, with Notes on Herman
> Melville, ed. Charles Roberts Anderson. Durham, N.C.: Duke
> University Press, 1937.

1936

8. Frankfurter, Edith. Die Südsee in der englischen und amerikanischen
Literature seit 1870 (Seit Melville und Stevenson): Roman und Lyrick.
University of Vienna, 1936. 243 pages.

> Brief mention is made of Melville's earlier works in the context of
> various other writers of the south seas.

9. Mansfield, Luther Stearns. Herman Melville; Author and New Yorker:
1844-1851. University of Chicago, 1936. 244 pages.

> The focus is on Melville's life, readings, and intellectual
> development during his early years as a writer.

> See: Mansfield, Luther Stearns. "Glimpses of Herman Melville's Life
> in Pittsfield, 1850-1851: Some Unpublished Letters of Evert A.
> Duyckinck," American Literature, 9 (March 1937), 26-48. "Melville's
> Comic Articles on Zachary Taylor," American Literature, 9 (January
> 1938), 411-18. "Melville and Hawthorne in the Berkshires," in
> Melville and Hawthorne in the Berkshires, ed. Howard P. Vincent,
> (Kent, Ohio: Kent State University Press, 1968), 4-21.

1937

10. Sundermann, Karl H. Herman Melvilles Gedankengut: Eine Kritische
Untersuchung seiner weltanschaulichen Grundlagen. Humboldt University
(Berlin), 1937.

See: Sundermann, Karl H. Herman Melvilles Gedankengut. Berlin:
Collignon, 1937.

11. Weber, Walter. Herman Melville, Eine Stilistische Untersuchung.
University of Basel, 1937.   ·

See: Weber, Walter. Herman Melville, Eine Stilistische Untersuchung.
Berlin: Polygraph, 1937.

1938

12. Simon, Jean. Herman Melville, l'Homme et l'Oeuvre. University of
Paris, 1938.

See: Simon, Jean. Herman Melville: Marin, Métaphysicien et Poète.
Paris: Boivin, 1939.

1939

13. Oliver, Egbert Samuel. Melville and the Idea of Progress.
University of Washington, 1939. 201 pages.

Melville's mind in the 1850's is given special treatment with chapters
on "Civilization and Polynesia," "Material Progress," "Social
Progress," and "Nature as Becoming."

1942

14. Foster, Elizabeth S. Herman Melville's The Confidence-Man: Its
Origins and Meaning. Yale University, 1942.

See: Foster, Elizabeth S. "Melville and Geology," American
Literature, 17 (March 1945), 50-65. "Another Note on Melville and
Geology," American Literature, 22 (January 1951), 479-87. The
Confidence-Man: His Masquerade, ed. Elizabeth S. Foster. New York:
Hendricks House, 1954.

15. Freeman, F. Barron. The Manuscripts of Herman Melville's Billy Budd.
Harvard University, 1942.

The manuscripts are documented and described.

See: Melville's Billy Budd, ed. F. Barron Freeman. Cambridge, Ma.:
Harvard University Press, 1948.

16. Kimpel, Ben Drew. <u>Herman Melville's Thought After 1851</u>. University of North Carolina at Chapel Hill, 1942. 520 pages.

Melville's later attitudes toward the major problems of existence, man's relation to God, man's nature, and his relation to other men are discussed.

See: Kimpel, Ben D. "Two Notes on Herman Melville," <u>American Literature</u>, 16 (March 1944), 29-32.

17. McEniry, William Hugh, Jr. <u>The Young Melville (1819-1852)</u>. Vanderbilt University, 1942. 234 pages.

Melville's experiences affected his philosophy and its expression in his major works leading up to <u>P</u>. An appendix contains a digest of the main interpretations of <u>MD</u>.

See: McEniry, W. Hugh. <u>The Young Melville</u>. Nashville, 1942.

18. Sealts, Merton M., Jr. <u>Herman Melville's Reading in Ancient Philosophy</u>. Yale University, 1942. 237 pages. Order 69-16,939.

Melville gathered knowledge of philosophers before the modern period through direct and second-hand reading. Here Plato and Socrates are closely viewed. (<u>DA</u>: 30-1574)

See: Sealts, Merton M., Jr. <u>Melville's Reading: A Checklist of Books Owned and Borrowed</u>. Madison, Wis.: University of Wisconsin Press, 1966. "A Supplementary Note to <u>Melville's Reading</u> (1966)," <u>Harvard Library Bulletin</u>, 19, 280-4. "A Second Supplementary Note to <u>Melville's Reading</u>," <u>Harvard Library Bulletin</u>, 27: 330-35. "Melville's 'Neoplatonic Originals,'" <u>Modern Language Notes</u>, 67 (February 1952), 80-86.

1943

19. Bezanson, Walter Everett. <u>Herman Melville's Clarel</u>. Yale University, 1943.

See: <u>Clarel: A Poem and a Pilgrimage in the Holy Land</u>, ed. Walter E. Bezanson, New York: Hendricks House, 1960.

20. Scott, Wilbur S., Jr. <u>Melville's Originality: A Study of Some of the Sources of Moby-Dick</u>. Princeton University, 1943. 295 pages. Order 3040.

Melville's whaling books and other minor sources are discussed in the order that they appear in "Cetology." (<u>DA</u>: 12-309)

1944

21. Hillway, Tyrus. Melville and Nineteenth-Century Science. Yale
University, 1944. 217 pages. Order 68-1307. (DA: 29-3578)

See: Hillway, Tyrus. "Melville and the Spirit of Science," South
Atlantic Quarterly, 48 (January 1949), 77-88. "Melville's Use of
Two Pseudo-Sciences," Modern Language Notes, 64 (March 1949), 145-50.
"Melville's Geological Knowledge," American Literature, 21 (May 1949),
232-237. Melville and the Whale. Stonington, Conn.: Stonington
Publishing Co., 1950. "Melville as Critic of Science," Modern
Language Notes, 65 (June 1950), 411-14. "Melville as Amateur
Zoologist," Modern Language Quarterly, 12 (June 1951), 159-64.

22. Roper, Gordon H. An Index of Herman Melville's Mardi, Moby-Dick,
Pierre, and Billy Budd. University of Chicago, 1944. 257 pages.

Listed are historical, fictional, and mythical persons; authors, books
plays, and poems; historical or imaginary places and events; and other
subjects mentioned by Melville in four major works. References are to
the Constable Edition.

1945

23. Culhane, Mary. Thoreau, Melville, Poe, and the Romantic Quest.
University of Minnesota, 1945. 437 pages.

Melville's "itch for the remote," a form of the romantic quest, leads
to a futile and on-going search for absolute truth, evident from M on.
HM: 104-240.

24. Hayford, Harrison M. Melville and Hawthorne: A Biographical and
Critical Study. Yale University, 1945. 387 pages.

Hitherto unpublished letters, original journal entries, and other
manuscript material serve as evidence in this chronological account
of Melville's relationship with Hawthorne. Discussed here are
"Mosses," Hawthorne's influence on MD, the "Agatha" letters, and
Melville's attempts at securing a consular appointment.

See: Hayford, Harrison. "The Significance of Melville's 'Agatha'
Letters," English Literary History, 13 (December 1946), 299-310.
"Hawthorne, Melville, and the Sea," New England Quarterly, 19
(December 1946), 435-52. and Merrell R. Davis. "Herman Melville as
Office Seeker," Modern Language Quarterly, 10 (June, September 1949),
168-83, 377-88.

1946

25. Pommer, Henry F. The Influence of Milton on Herman Melville. Yale University, 1946.

  See: Pommer, Henry F. Milton and Melville. Pittsburgh, Pa.: University of Pittsburgh Press, 1950.

26. Yaggy, Elinor. Pierre: Key to the Melville Enigma. University of Washington, 1946. 219 pages.

  P is an effort to compete with and yet satirize the cheap, sentimental novel of the time. Sources for the novel, Melville's purpose in writing it, and the problems of his literary silence subsequent to it are discussed.

  See: Yaggy, Elinor. "Shakespeare and Melville's Pierre," Boston Public Library Quarterly, 6 (January 1954), 43-51.

1947

27. Baird, James R. Herman Melville and Primitivism. Yale University, 1947.

  See: Baird, James R. Ishmael. Baltimore, Md.: Johns Hopkins Press, 1956; rpt. New York: Harper and Bros., 1960.

28. Davis, Merrell R. Herman Melville's Mardi: The Biography of a Book. Yale University, 1947.

  See: Davis, Merrell R. Melville's Mardi: A Chartless Voyage. New Haven, Conn.: Yale University Press, 1952; rpt. Hamden, Conn.: Archon Books, 1967.

29. Gilman, William H. Melville's Early Life and Redburn. Yale University, 1947.

  See: Gilman, William H. Melville's Early Life and Redburn. New York: New York University Press, 1951.

1948

30. Feidelson, Charles N., Jr. The Idea of Symbolism in American Writing, with Particular Reference to Ralph Waldo Emerson and Herman Melville. Yale University, 1948.

  See: Feidelson, Charles, Jr. Symbolism and American Literature. Chicago, Ill.: University of Chicago Press, 1953.

31. Haave, Ethel-Mae. Herman Melville's Pierre: A Critical Study. Yale University, 1948. 276 pages. Order 69-16,876.

P is not autobiography but a literary work. Examined here are Melville's intentions, his debts to his readings, his symbolism and communication of ideas. (DA: 30-1527)

1949

32. Barrett, Laurence N. Fiery Hunt: A Study in Melville's Theories of the Artist. Princeton University, 1949. 349 pages. Order 10,837.

Chapters discuss the development of Melville's theories of the artist from T to BB, symbolism, readings, and the concept of the brotherhood of authors. (DA: 15-410)

See: Barrett, Laurence. "The Differences in Melville's Poetry," PMLA, 70 (September 1955), 606-23.

33. Little, Thomas Alexander. Literary Allusions in the Writings of Herman Melville. University of Nebraska, 1949. 427 pages.

Allusions and their echoes throughout Melville's works are classified under such headings as Bible, literature, classical mythology and legend, literary personalities, and philosophy. The author's personality reflects the allusions he uses.

34. Wright, Nathalia. Herman Melville and the Bible. Yale University, 1949.

See: Wright, Nathalia. Melville's Use of the Bible. Durham, N.C.: Duke University Press, 1949.

1950

35. Morehead, Barbara. Melville's Use of the Narrator in Moby-Dick. University of Chicago, 1950. 228 pages.

Everything in MD is presented from the point of view of the first-person narrator over and above Ishmael. Melville's style is examined in terms of sentence structure, figures of speech, and sound devices. T and R are also discussed.

36. Scott, Sumner W. D. The Whale in Moby-Dick. University of Chicago, 1950. 258 pages.

Discussed here are the functions of the sections on the natural history of the sperm whale, of writers on whales, of whaling pictures, and of the classification of whales. An appendix compares texts from MD and Beale's Natural History of the Sperm Whale.

37. Thurman, Howard Kelly. <u>Herman Melville: Humanitarian and Critic of Politics</u>. University of Iowa, 1950. 183 pages.

Melville actively participated in political reforms. Chapters examine his awareness of the nation's political life, his references to reform from <u>T</u> to <u>BB</u>, and his protests against slavery and war as found in <u>M</u> and <u>BP</u>. Melville's ideal state is also discussed.

1951-1960

1951

38. Alderson, Edwin. L'Influence Française dans L'Oeuvre de Herman Melville. University of Toulouse, 1951.

39. Barry, Sister Marie of the Trinity. The Problem of Shifting Voice and Point of View in Melville's Early Novels and Moby-Dick. Catholic University of America, 1951. 174 pages.

> Narrative problems in MD are examined in terms of Melville's shifts from first-person to third-person point of view with emphasis on the place and nature of these shifts and the value of Melville's shifting.

40. Canfield, Francis X. Herman Melville's Vision of Conflict. University of Ottawa, 1951. 214 pages.

> Melville envisioned a stream of evil which marred all of God's creations. It is found in conflicts in society, within man himself, and between man and God. In BB, Melville accepts these conflicts as a basic part of creation.

> See: Canfield, Francis X. "Moby-Dick and the Book of Job," Catholic World, 174 (January 1952), 254-60.

41. Fiess, Edward. Byron and Byronism in the Mind and Art of Herman Melville. Yale University, 1951. 325 pages. Order 64-11,904.

> Byron's concern with philosophic questions, the role of the writer, and heroic Titanism directly influenced Melville from M to P. The latter work is the most Byronic. Afterwards, Melville grew more interested in Byron's life and satire. Also discussed are the affects of Calvinism on both men and Melville's reading of Byron's Life and Works. (DA: 25-4145)

> See: Fiess, Edward. "Melville as a Reader and Student of Byron," American Literature, 24 (May 1952), 186-94. "Byron's Dark Blue Ocean and Melville's Rolling Sea," English Language Notes, 3 (June 1966), 274-78.

42. Horsford, Howard C. Journal of a Visit to Europe and the Levant,
October 11, 1856 - May 6, 1857 by Herman Melville. Princeton University,
1951. 392 pages. Order 10,923.

Readers will find a full bibliography of nineteenth-century travel
literature and slightly fuller explanatory notes here than in
Horsford's published edition. (DA: 15-584)

See: Horsford, Howard C. "Evidence of Melville's Plans for a Sequel
to The Confidence-Man," American Literature, 24 (March 1952), 85-8.
Journal of a Visit to Europe and the Levant, October 11, 1856 - May 6,
1857, ed. Howard c. Horsford. Princeton, NJ: Princeton University
Press, 1955. (A revised edition will appear in volume fifteen of the
Northwestern-Newberry Writings of Herman Melville.) "Melville's
Journal of a Voyage to Europe and the Levant," American Literature.
28 (January 1957), 520-4.

43. Wolpert, Bernard Michael. The Melville Revival: A Study of
Twentieth-Century Criticism Through Its Treatment of Herman Melville.
Ohio State University, 1951. 298 pages. Order 25,480.

Chapters deal with the backgrounds of twentieth-century criticism;
British origins of the Melville revival; Melville and sociological,
psychological, philosophical, and pluralistic criticism; methods of
literary history, and the new criticism (DA: 18-1800)

1952

44. Creeger, George Raymond. Color Symbolism in the Works of Herman
Melville: 1846-1852. Yale University, 1952. 391 pages. Order 64-
11,897.

Melville uses color to produce irony, symbolic polarities and
dualities, and characterizations. (DA: 25-6620)

See: Creeger, George R. "The Symbolism of Whiteness in Melville's
Prose Fiction," Jahrbuch fur Amerikastudien, 5 (1960), 147-63.

45. Griffith, Frank Clark. Melville and the Quest for God. State
University of Iowa, 1952. 422 pages. Order 4064.

Melville's readings in Bayle and Montaigne acquainted him with
Pyrrhonist skepticism, which cuts man off from all certain knowledge
of God. As a result of this exposure, Melville's religious mind, in
its rebellion against the apparent evil of God, was forced into an
intellectual paradox that is the key to such writings as M, MD, P,
Clarel, and BB. (DA: 12-619)

46. Heflin, Wilson Lumpkin. Herman Melville's Whaling Years. Vanderbilt
University, 1952. 495 pages. Order 4397.

Melville's voyages on the Acushnet, Lucy Ann, and Charles and Henry
are examined along with factual sources for T and "The Town-Ho's
Story." (DA: 12-792)

See: Heflin, Wilson L. "The Sources of Ahab's Lordship Over the
Level Loadstone," American Literature, 20 (November 1948), 323-27.
"Melville's Third Whaler," Modern Language Notes, 64 (April 1949),
241-45. "Melville and Nantucket," Proceedings of the Nantucket
Historical Association, (1951), 22-30; rpt. in Moby-Dick Centennial
Essays, ed. Tyrus Hillway and Luther S. Mansfield, (Dallas, Tex:
Southern Methodist University Press, 1953), 165-79. "A Man-of-War
Button Divides Two Cousins," Boston Public Library Quarterly, 3
(January 1951), 51-60.

47. Hoffman, Charles George. The Development of the Short Novel in
Hawthorne, Melville, and James. University of Wisconsin, 1952.

Melville's use of the nouvelle after P reveals the development of the
author's creative capability, not its decline. HM: 109-202.

See: Hoffman, Charles G. "The Shorter Fiction of Herman Melville,"
South Atlantic Quarterly, 52 (July 1953), 414-30.

48. Nilon, Charles Hampton. Some Aspects of the Treatment of Negro
Characters by Five Representative American Novelists: Cooper, Melville,
Tourgée, Glasgow, Faulkner. University of Wisconsin, 1952. 499 pages.

In examining Pip, Fleece, and Babo, the study concludes that Melville
employs two themes in his treatment of blacks: God's tolerance of
evil and the ambiguity of appearance. HM: 56-113.

49. Runden, John Paul. Imagery in Melville's Shorter Fiction:
1853-1856. Indiana University, 1952. 221 pages. Order 4379.

Melville's imagery provides sensuous and metaphysical qualities and
serves as a structural device. Particular attention is given to the
paired stories and "Benito Cereno." (DA: 12-792)

50. Sweetser, Margaret Susan. Herman Melville's Conception of the Great
Writer and his Experiments in Literary Manners. University of Minnesota,
1952. 322 pages. Order 3658.

Melville's conceptions of literature and human experience are
discussed in light of his reportorial, humanitarian, and argumentative
uses of fact, and his heroic, epic, dramatic, and analytical manners
of writing. (DA: 12-311)

51. Walter, Josef. Herman Melville's Influence Upon F. Gerstäcker's
South Sea Novels. Fribourg, Switzerland, 1952.

1953

52. Aigner, Helmut. Die Entwicklung des Pessimismus in Prosawerk Herman
Melvilles. University of Vienna, 1953. 100 pages.

Although Melville was a pessimist throughout his life, his dark
philosophy changes throughout his works, in particular M, MD, P, and
BB. The study also compares Melville to the American naturalists.

53. Dibden, Arthur James. On the Religious Significance of Recent Interpretations of Promethean Tragedy. Columbia University, 1953. 186 pages. Order 6605.

  MD and BB are promethean tragedies. HM: 68-105. (DA: 14-192)

54. Fiske, John C. American Classics in Soviet Criticism. Harvard University, 1953.

  See: Fiske, John C. "Herman Melville in Soviet Criticism," Comparative Literature, 5 (Winter 1953), 30-39.

55. Key, Howard Cresap. The Influence of Travel Literature Upon Melville's Fictional Technique. Stanford University, 1953. 266 pages.

  In ascertaining Melville's attitude towards travel literature, this study argues that he used the material critically; it influenced his approach to literary problems.

56. Rosenberry, Edward H. The Comic Spirit in the Art of Herman Melville. University of Pennsylvania, 1953.

  See: Rosenberry, Edward H. Melville and the Comic Spirit. Cambridge, Ma.: Harvard University Press, 1955; rpt. New York: Octagon Press, 1969.

57. Stavig, Richard T. Melville's Billy Budd: A New Approach to the Problem of Interpretation. Princeton University, 1953. 269 pages. Order 8091.

  Drawing upon the 1842 Somers incident, the study argues that BB is not a "testament of acceptance." (DA: 14-822)

                              1954

58. Beharriell, Stanley Ross. The Head and the Heart in the Mind and Art of Herman Melville. University of Wisconsin, 1954. 455 pages.

  With special attention given to P, this study examines the ideas and symbols behind Melville's comment, "I stand for the heart. To dogs with the head!"

59. Betts, William W., Jr. The Fortunes of Faust in American Literature. Pennsylvania State University, 1954.

  Goethe influenced the creation of Ahab and MD as a whole. HM: 117-30.

  See: Betts, William W., Jr. "Moby-Dick: Melville's Faust," Lock Haven Bulletin, 1 (1959), 31-44.

60. Clavering, Rose. The Conflict Between the Individual and Social Forces in Herman Melville's Works: Typee to Moby-Dick. New York University, 1954. 494 pages. Order 22,941.

The problems of the needs and rights of the individual as opposed to those of society are discussed in economic, political, religious, and interpersonal contexts. (DA: 18-2137)

61. Hoffman, Leonard Raymond. Problems in Melville: The Style from the Beginning through Moby-Dick. Stanford University, 1954. 292 pages. Order 10,374.

Each work preceding MD solves or fails to solve technical problems in exposition, sequence, narrative process, and character. (DA: 14-2346)

62. Moriarty, Jane Viva. The American Novel in France, 1919-1939. University of Wisconsin, 1954.

Melville's favorable reception in France between the World Wars is due to his works' escape to the exotic and their assurance of significance in human activity. HM: 72-89.

63. Sperling, Helmut. Herman Melville als Kritiker Seiner Zeit. Humboldt University (Berlin), 1954. 167 pages.

1955

64. Gross, John J. Herman Melville and the Search for Community. State University of Iowa, 1955. 330 pages. Order 12,895.

For Melville and some of his European contemporaries (especially Dostoevsky), literature is a search for community. From M to P, Melville discovered that embracing absolute idealism resulted in self-annihilation and loss of vital interpersonal relationships. His major focus from BP to BB was on theistic (rather than humanistic) ideas of community. (DA: 15-1619)

See: Gross, John J. "The Rehearsal of Ishmael: Melville's Redburn," Virginia Quarterly Review, 27 (Autumn 1951), 581-600. "Melville, Dostoevsky, and the People," Pacific Spectator, 10 (Spring 1956), 160-70. "The Writer in America--A Search for Community," Queen's Quarterly, 63 (Autumn 1956), 375-91. "Religion and Community in the American Renaissance," Emerson Society Quarterly, 44 (III Q 1966), 59-64.

65. Helmcke, Hans. Die Funktion des Ich-Erzahlers in Herman Melvilles Roman Moby-Dick. University of Mainz, 1955.

See: Helmcke, Hans. Die Funktion des Ich-Erzahlers in Herman Melvilles Roman Moby-Dick mit einem vergleichenden Blick auf Melvilles frühere Romane. München: Max Hueber, 1957.

66. Hitt, Ralph E. <u>Controversial Poetry of the Civil War Period:</u>
<u>1830-1878</u>. Vanderbilt University, 1955. 474 pages. Order 15,796.

Although both Melville and Whitman hoped to effect a sympathetic
understanding between North and South, Melville displays a more
moderate and objective view of war and reconstruction. HM: 182-87,
244-62. (<u>DA</u>: 16-537)

See: Hitt, Ralph E. "Melville's Poems of the Civil War Controversy,"
<u>Studies in the Literary Imagination</u>, 2 (April 1969), 57-68.

67. O'Daniel, Therman Benjamin. <u>A Study of Melville's Journals,</u>
<u>Lectures, and Letters</u>. University of Ottawa, 1955. 367 pages.

Although largely an analysis of the letters, this thesis discusses
Melville's use of the journals in both prose and verse and speculates
on the contents of Melville's lectures and the reason for his failure
as a lecturer.

See: O'Daniel, Therman B. "Herman Melville as a Writer of Journals,"
<u>College Language Association Journal</u>, 4 (December 1960), 94-105.

68. Stern, Milton Ralph. <u>Theme and Craft in Herman Melville: Fine</u>
<u>Hammered Steel</u>. Michigan State University, 1955. 436 pages. Order
12,958. (<u>DA</u>: 15-1859)

See: Stern, Milton R. <u>The Fine Hammered Steel of Herman Melville</u>.
Champaign, Ill.: University of Illinois Press, 1957.

1956

69. Bennett, John Frederic. <u>Melville's Humanitarian Thought: A Study in</u>
<u>Moral Idealism</u>. University of Wisconsin, 1956. 583 pages. Order 16,143.

An analysis of the works (<u>MD</u> in particular) shows how the theme of
humanitarianism relates to the actions of Melville's characters.
(<u>DA</u>: 16-961)

70. Fite, Olive Larue. <u>The Interpretation of Melville's Billy Budd</u>.
Northwestern University, 1956. 369 pages. Order 18,984.

Discussed here are the sources for <u>BB</u>, Melville's markings in books
read at the time of the short novel's composition, other writings of
the period, and <u>BB</u> criticism. (<u>DA</u>: 17-354)

See: Fite, Olive L. "Billy Budd, Claggart, and Schopenhauer,"
<u>Nineteenth-Century Fiction</u>, 23 (December 1968), 336-43.

71. Rasco, Lavon. <u>The Biographies of Herman Melville: A Study in</u>
<u>Twentieth-Century Biography</u>. Northwestern University, 1956. 296 pages.
Order 19,032.

Each biography presents a different Melville. The problem of why and
how biographies differ is explored by examining each work in a

chronological sequence, the use to which each biographer put the available data, and each biography's historical framework. (DA: 17-357)

72. Vogel, Dan. Melville's Shorter Published Poetry: A Critical Study of the Lyrics in Mardi, of Battle-Pieces, John Marr, and Timoleon. New York University, 1956. 319 pages. Order 18,069.

In assessing the literary value of Melville's shorter poetry, the study compares the symbology of short verses to that of the prose in which they appear. (DA: 17-367)

See: Vogel, Dan. "Note: 'The Coming Storm,'" Melville Society Newsletter, 11 (Summer 1955), 2-3.

1957

73. Bowen, Merlin. Self and Experience in the Writings of Herman Melville. University of Chicago, 1957.

See: Bowen, Merlin. The Long Encounter: Self and Experience in the Writings of Herman Melville. Chicago, Ill.: University of Chicago Press, 1960.

74. Canaday, Nicholas, Jr. Melville and Authority: A Study of Thematic Unity. University of Florida, 1957.

See: Canady, Nicholas, Jr. "A New Reading of Melville's 'Benito Cereno,'" in Studies in American Literature, ed. Waldo McNeir and Leo B. Levy, (Baton Rouge, La.: Louisiana State University Press, 1960), 49-57. "The Theme of Authority in Melville's Typee and Omoo," Forum, 4 (Fall 1963), 38-41. Melville and Authority. Gainesville, Fla.: University of Florida Press, 1968. "Melville's Pierre: At War with the Social Convention," Papers on English Literature and Language, 5 (Winter 1969), 51-62.

75. Farnsworth, Robert M. Melville's Use of Point of View in his First Seven Novels. Tulane University, 1957. 215 pages. Order 59-666.

Melville's skill as a literary craftsman and his thought develop through the early works. (DA: 19-3294)

See: Farnsworth, Robert M. "Ishmael to the Royal Masthead," University of Kansas City Review, 28 (Spring 1962), 183-90. "From Voyage to Quest in Melville," Emerson Society Quarterly, 28 (III Q 1962), 17-20.

76. Finkelstein, Dorothee Grdseloff. Herman Melville and the Near East. Yale University, 1957.

See: Finkelstein, Dorothee Metlitsky. Melville's Orienda. New Haven, Conn.: Yale University Press, 1961.

77. Foster, Edward Francis. A Study of Grim Humor in the Works of Poe, Melville, and Twain. Vanderbilt University, 1957. 305 pages. Order 22,012.

The nature and manner of Melville's grim humor develops from plain joking to atmospheric and thematic importance. HM: 137-213. (DA: 17-1761)

78. Mahoney, Mother M. Denis. Clarel: An Investigation of Spiritual Crisis. Catholic University of America, 1957.

Clarel poses two questions: "Whose the eye that sees aright if any?" and "What may man know?"

For abstract, See: Mahoney, Mother M. Denis. Clarel: An Investigation of Spiritual Crisis. Washington, D.C.: Catholic University of America Press, 1958.

79. O'Donnell, Charles Robert. The Mind of the Artist: Cooper, Thoreau, Hawthorne, Melville. Syracuse University, 1957. 187 pages. Order 21,923.

In M, WJ, and BB, Melville portrays the artist's disillusionment, journey toward new knowledge, and final return to the community of mankind. HM: 146-80. (DA: 17-1752)

                              1958

80. Battenfield, David Hatch. I Seek for Truth: A Comparative Study of Melville's Moby-Dick and Pierre. Stanford University, 1958. 128 pages. Order 58-1279.

The plots, themes, and major characters reveal both books to be Melville's artistic search for the self. (DA: 18-1426)

See: Battenfield, David H. "The Source for the Hymn in Moby-Dick," American Literature, 27 (November 1955), 393-96.

81. Davies, James William. The Vision of Evil: An Inquiry into the Dialog Between Emerson, Melville, Hawthorne, and the Nineteenth Century. Union Theological Seminary in the City of New York, 1958.

Such forces as commercialism, revivalism, industrialism, optimism, and democracy erode the strict Puritan vision of evil with which American culture began. Emerson attempted to revivify the materialism of his age by infusing it with a sense of beauty and spirit, but in doing so failed to sharpen his sensibility to a vision of evil. Melville, however, in his early novels is a "propagandist" for a darker view of Christianity and the nation. In MD, the problems of evil reside in personality society and culture, and metaphysics. BB reveals Melville's attachment to a goodness borne out of "genuine Christianity" which is continually eroded by the evils of civilization. Melville, then, is essentially a Rousseauean. HM: 99-185.

82. Van, Lê. <u>Herman Melville, Romancier Polynésien et Maritime</u>. Aix en Marseille, 1958. 224 pages. (<u>Deal</u> 1968)

1959

83. Ballenger, Sara Elizabeth. <u>The Reception of the American Novel in German Periodicals (1945-1957)</u>. Indiana University, 1959. 167 pages. Order 59-3986.

Melville was rediscovered in 1944 and positively received thereafter. HM: 48-56. (<u>DA</u>: 20-1360)

84. Boies, Jack Jay. <u>Herman Melville: Nihilist</u>. University of Wisconsin, 1959. 695 pages. Order 59-3240.

After his disillusionment, Melville turned his desire for belief into destructivity. Separate sections treat Melville's resultant personal, social, and metaphysical despair. (<u>DA</u>: 20-1022)

See: Boies, Jack Jay. "Existential Nihilism and Herman Melville," <u>Transactions of the Wisconsin Academy</u>, 50 (1961), 307-20. "The Whale Without Epilogue," <u>Modern Language Quarterly</u>, 24 (June 1963), 172-76. "Melville's Quarrel with Angelicanism," <u>Emerson Society Quarterly</u>, 33 (IV Q 1963), 75-79.

85. Humbach, Anne. <u>Aspekte der Wortbildung bei Herman Melville</u>. Freiberg im Breisgau, 1959. 181 pages.

86. Kaplan, Sidney. <u>Herman Melville and the American National Sin</u>. Harvard University, 1959. 287 pages.

Slavery is treated chronologically in Melville's writings and ideas.

See: Kaplan, Sidney. "Herman Melville and the American National Sin: The Meaning of 'Benito Cereno,'" <u>Journal of Negro History</u>, 41 (October 1956), 311-38; 42 (January 1957), 11-37; rpt. in <u>Images of the Negro in American Literature</u>, ed. Seymour L. Gross and John Edward Hardy, (Chicago: University of Chicago Press, 1966), 135-62.

87. Mangold, Charlotte Weiss. <u>Herman Melville in German Criticism from 1900 to 1955</u>. University of Maryland, 1959. 417 pages. Order 60-1281.

Extensive quotations from German critics indicate how widely Melville was known in that country and what attitudes were held. (<u>DA</u>: 20-4114)

88. Shulman, Robert Philip. <u>Toward Moby-Dick: Melville and Some Baroque Worthies</u>. Ohio State University, 1959. 383 pages. Order 60-794.

<u>MD</u> (Ishmael, Stubb, and Starbuck in particular) shows stylistic resemblances (verbal echoes and organizing patterns) to Rabelais, Plutarch, Montaigne, Browne, and Thomas Fuller. (<u>DA</u>: 20-3731)

See: Shulman, Robert. "The Serious Function of Melville's Phallic
Jokes," American Literature, 33 (May 1961), 179-94. "Melville's
Thomas Fuller: An Outline for Starbuck and an Instance of the Creator
as Critic," Modern Language Quarterly, 23 (December 1962), 337-52.
"Montaigne and the Technique and Tragedy of Melville's Billy Budd,"
Comparative Literature, 16 (Fall 1964), 322-30. "Melville's
'Timoleon': From Plutarch to the Early Stages of Billy Budd,"
Comparative Literature, 19 (Fall 1967), 351-61.

89. Ward, Joseph Thomas. Herman Melville: The Forms and Forces of Evil.
University of Notre Dame, 1959. 333 pages. Order 59-6574.

Bayle and Hawthorne influenced Melville's use of occult and
diabolistic themes throughout the major fiction. (DA: 20-2786)

90. Zeik, Michael. The Traditional Element in Herman Melville's Thought
with Special Attention to Clarel. Georgetown University, 1959. 317
pages.

Clarel demonstrates great respect for Judaeo-Christian traditions and
the Roman Catholic Church in particular. Emphasis is given to Father
Mapple's sermon, Rousseau, and the Jacksonian era.

1960

91. Hoyle, Norman Eugene. Melville as a Magazinist. Duke University,
1960. 262 pages. Order 60-6244.

Melville's contributions to magazines and his possible authorship of
anonymous pieces in the Literary World are explored. (DA: 21-2295)

92. Jarrard, Norman Eugene. Poems by Herman Melville: A Critical
Edition of the Published Verse. University of Texas, 1960. 415 pages.
Order 60-6623.

This edition includes variorum textual notes on all poems published
by Melville (excluding Clarel). Copy texts for John Marr and Timoleon
are established from manuscript. The study also discusses Melville's
method of preparing a text and his editorial influences. (DA:
21-2714)

93. Nault, Clifford A., Jr. Melville's Two-Stranded Novel: An Interpre-
tation of Moby-Dick as an Enactment of Father Mapple's Sermon and the
Lesser Prophecies, with an Essay on Melville Interpretation. Wayne State
University, 1960. 286 pages. Order 60-2332.

Father Mapple's sermon connects two plots in MD associated with two
Ishmaels--the narrator and the participant. (DA: 22-1979)

94. Plumstead, Arthur William. Time's Endless Tunnel: A Study of Herman
Melville's Concern with Time. University of Rochester, 1960. 360 pages.

Time is a major motif in Melville's works; references to it in the
public and private writings are discussed chronologically.

1961-1970

1961

95. Bernstein, John Albert. <u>Pacificism and Rebellion in the Writings of Herman Melville</u>. University of Pennsylvania, 1961. 290 pages. Order 62-281. (<u>DA</u>: 23-221)

    See: Bernstein, John. "'Benito Cereno'" and the Spanish Inquisition," <u>Nineteenth-Century Fiction</u>, 16 (March 1962), 345-50. <u>Pacificism and Rebellion in the Writings of Herman Melville</u>. The Hague: Mouton, 1964.

96. Franklin, Howard Bruce. <u>Melville's Mythology</u>. Stanford University, 1961. 243 pages. Order 62-301. (<u>DA</u>: 22-3644)

    See: Franklin, H. Bruce. "'Apparent Symbol of Despotic Command': Melville's 'Benito Cereno,'" <u>New England Quarterly</u>, 34 (December 1961), 462-77. <u>The Wake of the Gods: Melville's Mythology</u>. Stanford, Ca.: Stanford University Press, 1963.

97. Hall, Joan Joffe. <u>Some Problems of Structure in Melville's Novels</u>. Stanford University, 1961. 203 pages. Order 62-305.

    The image of the voyage reflects Melville's changing attitudes. His alternation of action with interpolation is a means by which Melville interprets, prefigures, and parallels the central action. (<u>DA</u>: 22-3663)

    See: Hall, Joan Joffe. "Historical Chapters in <u>Billy Budd</u>," <u>University Review</u>, 30 (Autumn 1963), 35-40. "Melville's Use of Interpolations," <u>University Review</u>, 33 (October 1966), 51-59.

98. Hayman, Allen. <u>Herman Melville's Theory of Prose Fiction: In Contrast with Contemporary Theories</u>. University of Illinois at Champaign, 1961. 274 pages. Order 61-1620.

    After examining the prose theories found in seven American periodicals between 1844 and 1857, the study discusses Melville's theory and practice as they correspond to Hawthorne's preference for "vital truth" over surface verisimilitude. (<u>DA</u>: 21-3782)

See: Hayman, Allen. "The Real and the Original: Herman Melville's Theory of Prose Fiction," Modern Fiction Studies, 8 (Autumn 1962), 211-32.

99. Kosok, Heinz. Die Bedeutung der Gothic Novel für das Erzählwerk Herman Melvilles. University of Marburg, 1961.

See: Kosok, Heinz, Die Bedeutung der Gothic Novel für das Erzählwerk Herman Melvilles. Hamburg: Cram, de Gruyter, 1963.

100. Lindgren, Charlotte Holt. The Common Seaman in Nineteenth Century American Fiction. Boston University, 1961. 277 pages. Order 61-1103.

Seen in the light of contemporary writing on the sea and Melville's early works (O, R, and WJ, in particular), MD is the apex of the sea-frontier myth. (DA: 22-872)

101. Rosenfeld, William. The Divided Burden: Common Elements in the Search for a Religious Synthesis in the Works of Theodore Parker, Horace Bushnell, Nathaniel Hawthorne, and Herman Melville. University of Minnesota, 1961. 245 pages. Order 62-1843.

The themes of human potentiality and limitation, faith and reason, social and asocial urges, and the need for an overriding religious consciousness are explored. (DA: 22-4019)

See: Rosenfeld, William. "Uncertain Faith: Queequeg's Coffin and Melville's Use of the Bible," Texas Studies in Literature and Language, 7 (Winter 1966), 317-27.

102. Seelye, John Douglas. The Iridescent Scabbard: Melville's Ironic Mode. Claremont Graduate School, 1961. 526 pages. Order 62-1231. (DA: 23-226)

See: Seelye, John D. "The Ironic Diagram" in The Recognition of Herman Melville, ed. Hershel Parker (Ann Arbor, Mi.: University of Michigan Press, 1967), 347-64. "The Golden Navel: The Cabalism of Ahab's Doubloon," Nineteenth-Century Fiction, 14 (1960), 350-55. Melville: The Ironic Diagram. Evanston, Ill.: Northwestern University Press, 1970.

103. Weeks, Lewis Ernest, Jr. American and British Periodical Criticism of Certain Nineteenth Century American Authors, 1840-1860. Boston University, 1961. 482 pages. Order 61-3411.

The study covers every book from T to CM. HM: 303-71. (DA: 22-1164)

103.5 Yeager, Henry. La Fortune Littéraire d'Herman Melville en France. University of Paris, 1961. 231 pages.

See: Yeager, Henry J. "Melville's Literary Debut in France," Midwest Quarterly, 11 (July 1970), 413-25. La fortune littéraire d'Herman Melville en France. Liège Presses Universitaires de Liège, 1970.

1962

104. Eckardt, Sister Mary Ellen, I.H.M. An Interpretive Analysis of the Patterns of Imagery in Moby-Dick and Billy Budd. University of Notre Dame, 1962. 337 pages. Order 63-290.

Image patterns in MD are discussed in terms of psychology, myth, and metaphysics. The dominant pattern in BB is the average man's limitation in distinguishing between appearance and reality. (DA: 28-2134)

See: Eckardt, Sister Mary Ellen, I.H.M. "Duplicate Imagery in Moby-Dick," Modern Fiction Studies, 8 (Autumn 1962), 252-64. "Parallels in Contrast: A Study of Melville's Imagery in Moby-Dick and Billy Budd," Studies in Short Fiction, 2 (Spring 1965), 284-90.

105. Jones, Walter Dickinson. A Critical Study of Herman Melville's Israel Potter. University of Alabama, 1962. 134 pages. Order 63-3659.

IP develops along four lines: the adventure, the historical tale, comedy, and symbol or allegory. (DA: 23-4357)

106. Knapp, Joseph George, S.J. Tortured Torturer of Reluctant Rhymes: Melville's Clarel, an Interpretation of Post-Civil War America. University of Minnesota, 1962. 268 pages. Order 63-7967. (DA: 24-2035)

See: Knapp, Joseph G., S. J. "Melville's Clarel: Dynamic Synthesis." American Transcendental Quarterly, 7 (Summer 1970), 67-76. Tortured Synthesis: The Meaning of Melville's Clarel. New York: Philosophical Library Press, 1971.

107. McCarthy, Paul Eugene. Theme and Structure in the Novels of Herman Melville. University of Texas, 1962. 280 pages. Order 62-2561.

Separate chapters discuss Melville's fiction as adventure, drama, or symbolic novel. (DA: 23-237)

See: McCarthy, Paul E. "The 'Soldier of Fortune' in Melville's The Confidence-Man," Emerson Society Quarterly, 33 (IV Q 1963), 21-4. "Character and Structure in Billy Budd," Discourse, 9 (Spring 1966), 201-17. "Symbolic Elements in White-Jacket," Midwest Quarterly, (Summer 1966), 309-25. "Affirmative Elements in The Confidence-Man," American Transcendental Quarterly, 7 (Summer 1970), 56-61.

108. Rosen, Roma. Melville's Uses of Shakespeare's Plays. Northwestern University, 1962. 257 pages. Order 63-1343.

After a discussion of Melville's critical comments on and markings of Shakespeare, the study focuses on Melville's uses of the plays in MD and P and concludes with a review of the author's indebtedness to the Bible, Milton, and Shakespeare. (DA: 23-3356)

109. Yamaya, Saburo. Reinterpretation of Herman Melville's Works: From Moby-Dick to The Confidence-Man. Kyushu University, 1962.

1963

110. Beck, Betty Shrock. <u>The Fallible Narrator in Nineteenth Century</u>
<u>American Fiction</u>. University of Oklahoma, 1963. 303 pages. Order
63-6703.

    The theme of appearance and reality appears throughout Melville's work
    especially in "Benito Cereno." HM: 137-66. (<u>DA</u>: 24-1610)

111. Blackburn, A. L. <u>The Picaresque Novel, A Literary Idea, 1554-1954</u>.
Fitzwilliam College, Cambridge University, 1963.

112. Blansett, Barbara Ruth Nieweg. <u>Melville and Emersonian Transcendent-</u>
<u>ialism</u>. University of Texas, 1963. 210 pages. Order 64-42.

    Early on, Melville was attracted to Emerson's transcendental ideals as
    revealed in the <u>Essays</u>. The author's transition to an anti-transcend-
    ental position culminates in <u>P</u>. (<u>DA</u>: 24-2904)

    See: Blansett, Barbara Nieweg. "'From Dark to Dark': <u>Mardi</u>, A Fore-
    shadowing of <u>Pierre</u>," <u>Southern Quarterly</u>, 1 (April 1963), 213-27.

113. Brodtkorb, Paul, Jr. <u>Herman Melville's Symbology</u>. Yale University,
1963.

    See: Brodtkorb, Paul, Jr. <u>Ishmael's White World: A Phenomenological</u>
    <u>Reading of Moby-Dick</u>. New Haven, Conn.: Yale University Press, 1965.

114. Ehrlich, Heyward Bruce. <u>A Study of Literary Activity in New York</u>
<u>City During the 1840-Decade</u>. New York University, 1963. 485 pages. Order
66-5625.

    Melville was linked to the Democratic journals of the 1840's through
    his brother Gansevoort and was sympathetic to the expansionism and
    literary nationalism of the Young America Movement. (<u>DA</u>: 27-201)

    See: Ehrlich, Heyward. "A Note on Melville's 'Men Who Dive,'"
    <u>Bulletin of the New York Public Library</u>, 69 (December 1965), 661-4.
    "'Diving and Ducking Moralities': A Rejoinder," <u>Bulletin of the New</u>
    <u>York Public Library</u>, 70 (November 1966), 552-3.

115. Grenberg, Bruce Leonard. <u>Thomas Carlyle and Herman Melville:</u>
<u>Parallels, Obliques, and Perpendiculars</u>. University of North Carolina at
Chapel Hill, 1963. 351 pages. Order 64-1851.

    From <u>T</u> to <u>P</u>, Melville's expression and style was influenced by Carlyle.
    This study is organized along the lines of basic ideological concepts
    shared by both and evaluates those instances in which Melville reacted
    against Carlyle and formulated his own positions. (<u>DA</u>: 24-3323)

116. Hinchcliffe, A.P. Symbolism in the American Novel, 1850-1950: An Examination of the Findings of Recent Literary Critics in Respect of Hawthorne, Melville, James, Hemingway, and Faulkner. University of Manchester, 1963.

> Building from Feidelson, this study shows how Melville uses his experiences symbolically in MD, P, and BB. Hawthorne's possible influence is discussed. HM: 142-294.

117. Kreuter, Kent Kirby. The Literary Response to Science, Technology, and Industrialism: Studies in the Thought of Hawthorne, Melville, Whitman, and Twain. University of Wisconsin, 1963. 316 pages. Order 64-652.

> Melville expresses compassion for technology's victims and a nostalgia for quality's sacrifice to the machine. For Melville, the artist is inevitably alienated from a society devoted to material progress. HM: 70-161. (DA: 24-2446)

118. Lucas, Thomas Edward. Herman Melville as Literary Theorist. University of Denver, 1963. 164 pages. Order 63-7847.

> Discussed here are Melville's views of final, efficient, material, and formal causes of art; characterization, and the function of art. (DA: 24-2015)

> See: Lucas, T.E. "Herman Melville: The Purpose of the Novel," Texas Studies in Literature and Language, 13 (Winter 1972), 641-61.

119. Packard, Robert Joslin. A Study of Herman Melville's Clarel. Columbia University, 1963. 244 pages. Order 63-7426.

> Metaphysical doubt, narrative technique, and thematic emphasis are discussed in chapters which include charts of the narrative, character sketches and maps for each of the poem's four sections. (DA: 24-2018)

120. Parker, Hershel. Melville and Politics: A Scrutiny of the Political Milieux of Herman Melville's Life and Works. Northwestern University, 1963. 329 pages. Order 64-5862.

> Hitherto unpublished letters, papers, and diaries of Melville's relatives and friends, previously unused political pamphlets and histories, and newly-discovered newspaper articles serve as evidence for the author's political attitudes and ideas. (DA: 24-5390)

> See: Parker, Hershel. "Gansevoort Melville's Role in the Campaign of 1844," New York Historical Society Quarterly, 49 (April 1965), 143-73. "Gansevoort Melville's 1846 London Journal," Bulletin of the New York Public Library, 69 (December 1965), 632-54; 70 (January, February 1966), 36-49, 113-31.

121. Zimmerman, Michael P, Herman Melville in the 1920's: A Study in the Origins of the Melville Revival, with an Annotated Bibliography. Columbia University, 1963. 231 pages. Order 64-9219.

> The focus here is on the two early revivals (1890's and 1910's), the direction of the criticism in the 1920's, the reasons for the revival's

success, and its significance. Back matter includes an annotated bibliography and list of Melville reprints from 1847 to 1929. (<u>DA</u>: 25-1224)

See: Zimmerman, Michael. "Herman Melville in the 1920's: An Annotated Bibliography," <u>Bulletin of Bibliography</u>, 24 (September-December 1964; January-April 1965), 117-20, 106; 139-44. "Literary Revivalism in America: Some Notes Toward a Hypothesis," <u>American Quarterly</u>, 19 (Spring 1967), 71-85.

1964

122. Elliott, Patrick F. <u>Melville's Tragic Vision: An Essay in Theological Criticism</u>. University of Chicago, 1964. 185 pages.

Kierkegaard allows us a Christian theological interpretation of <u>T</u>, <u>R</u>, <u>WJ</u>, <u>MD</u>, and <u>BB</u>.

123. Guetti, James Lawrence, Jr. <u>The Failure of the Imagination: A Study of Melville, Conrad, and Faulkner</u>. Cornell University, 1964. 240 pages. Order 64-13,805. (<u>DA</u>: 25-4145)

See: Guetti, James. <u>The Limits of Metaphor: A Study of Melville, Conrad, and Faulkner</u>. Ithaca, N.Y.: Cornell University Press, 1967.

124. Gupta, Raj Kumar. <u>Form and Style in Herman Melville's Pierre: Or the Ambiguities</u>. University of Pittsburgh, 1964. 159 pages. Order 65-5209.

Examined here are Pierre's role as tragic hero and the book's use of expository, analytical-reflective, and dramatic styles, of epic and dramatic conventions, and of symbolism and imagery. (<u>DA</u>: 26-1631)

See: Gupta, R. K. "Imagery in Melville's <u>Pierre</u>," <u>Kyushu American Literature</u>, 10 (1967), 41-49. "Melville's Use of Non-Novelistic Conventions in <u>Pierre</u>," in <u>Indian Essays in American Literature: Papers in Honour of Robert E. Spiller</u>, ed. Sujit Mukherjee and D. V. K. Raghavacharyulu, (Bombay: Popular Prakashan, 1969), 121-28.

125. Keller, Karl. <u>The Metaphysical Strain in Nineteenth-Century American Poetry</u>. University of Minnesota, 1964. 230 pages. Order 65-15,231.

Like Thoreau, Emerson, and Dickinson, Melville borrows the individualism, ingenuity, and meditative vision of the metaphysical poets. In particular, Melville is indebted to Emerson and Thomas Browne. HM: 154-74. (<u>DA</u>: 26-4631)

126. Kitch, John C. <u>Dark Laughter: A Study of the Pessimistic Tradition in American Humor</u>. Northwestern University, 1964. 814 pages. Order 65-3285.

Melville's humor is dark. HM: 83-160. (<u>DA</u>: 25-6595)

127. Lebowitz, Alan Louis. Melville's Ahab: The Evolution and Extinction of the Hero. Harvard University, 1964.

See: Lebowitz, Alan. Progress into Silence: A Study of Melville's Heroes. Bloomington, In.: Indiana University Press, 1970.

128. Magaw, Malcolm Orrin. Melville and the Christian Myth: The Imagery of Ambiguity. Tulane University, 1964. 327 pages. Order 64-13,708.

That Melville's creative method is more symbolistic than allegorical can be seen in the fact that the author is his own myth-maker and his meanings arise out of an organic pattern of development within his imagery rather than out of preconceptions imposed upon it. (DA: 25-4126)

See: Magaw, Malcolm O. "The Confidence-Man and Christian Deity: Melville's Imagery of Ambiguity," in Explorations of Literature, ed. Rima Drell Reck, (Baton Rouge, La.: Louisiana State University Press, 1966), 81-99. "Apocalyptic Imagery in Melville's 'The Apple-Tree Table,'" Midwest Quarterly, 8 (July 1967), 357-69.

129. Meldrum, Barbara Howard. Melville's Mardi, Moby-Dick, and Pierre: Tragedy in Recoil. Claremont Graduate School, 1964. 302 pages. Order 66-3344.

The three novels are discussed in terms of their tragic structures, heroes, points of view, and ramifications for the creative artist. (DA: 28-686)

See: Meldrum, Barbara. "Melville on War," Research Studies, a Quarterly Publication of Washington State University, 37 (June 1969), 130-38. "The Artist in Melville's Mardi," Studies in the Novel, 1 (Winter 1969), 459-67.

130. Newbery, Ilse Sofie Magdalene. The Imagery of Melville's Piazza Tales. University of British Columbia, 1964. 344 pages. Order 65-4534.

Both CM and PT reveal Melville's awareness of evil as a disintegrating force resulting in a new detachment bordering on moral nihilism. The tales, then, do not move in the direction of acceptance, and "The Piazza" emphasizes man's irredeemable aloneness. (DA: 26-4668)

See: Newbery, I. "'The Encantadas': Melville's Inferno," American Literature, 38 (March 1966), 49-68.

131. Star, Morris. Melville's Use of the Visual Arts. Northwestern University, 1964. 242 pages. Order 64-11,260.

Melville's aesthetic theory develops through three phases of concentration: a facade of verisimilitude, an avowal of organic form and inspiration, and a late homage to classicism. He uses pictorial images in five ways: as sources of factual information, foreshadowing devices, reinforcements of concreteness, aids to exhalt and intensify, and symbols. (DA: 25-2988)

See: Star, Morris. "A Checklist of Portraits of Herman Melville,"
<u>Bulletin of the New York Public Library</u>, 71 (Summer 1967), 468-73.
"Melville's Markings in Walpole's <u>Anecdotes of Painting in England</u>,"
<u>Papers of the Bibliographical Society of America</u>, 66 (III Q 1972),
321-7.

1965

132. Camp, James Edwin. <u>An Unfulfilled Romance: Image, Symbol, and
Allegory in Herman Melville's Clarel</u>. University of Michigan, 1965. 181
pages. Order 66-6579.

"The Paradise of Bachelors and the Tartarus of Maids" is the key to the
gnostic patterns in <u>Clarel</u>. The sea-desert analogy is the poem's basic
metaphoric frame. (<u>DA</u>: 27-472)

133. Charters, Ann. <u>Writers in a Landscape: Seven Writers in the
Berkshires, 1816-1917</u>. Columbia University, 1965. 154 pages. Order
66-4765.

In contrast to Hawthorne, Melville (especially in <u>P</u>) depended heavily
"on his environment to give substance to his concern with moral
allegory." HM: 90-109. (<u>DA</u>: 27-199)

134. Cowen, Wilson Walker. <u>Melville's Marginalia</u>. Harvard University,
1965. 5,498 pages.

Melville's markings and annotations in his books have biographical and
literary importance. The thesis reproduces these markings in type-
script.

See: Cowen, Walker. "Melville's 'Discoveries': A Dialogue of the
Mind with Itself," in <u>The Recognition of Herman Melville</u>, ed. Hershel
Parker, (Ann Arbor, Mi.: University of Michigan Press, 1967), 333-46.

135. Dryden, Edgar Afton. <u>Herman Melville's Narrators and the Art of
Fiction: A Study in Point of View</u>. Johns Hopkins University, 1965. 341
pages. Order 65-10,272. (<u>DA</u>: 26-3298)

See: Dryden, Edgar A. <u>Melville's Thematics of Form: The Great Art
of Telling the Truth</u>. Baltimore, Md.: Johns Hopkins University
Press, 1968.

136. Ensslen, Klaus. <u>Stil- und strukturanalytische Untersuchungen von
Herman Melvilles Tales (Einschliesslich Billy Budd)</u>. University of Munich,
1965.

See: Ensslen, Klaus. <u>Melvilles Erzahlungen, stil-und
strukturanalytische Untersuchungen</u>. Heidelberg: Carl Winter, 1966.

137. Frank, Max. Die Farb- un Lichtsymbolik im Prosawerk Herman
Melvilles. University of Tübingen, 1965.

   See: Frank, Max. Die Farb- und Lichtsymbolik im Prosawerk Herman
   Melvilles. Heidelberg: Carl Winter, 1967.

138. Hoar, Victor Myers, Jr. The Confidence Man in American Literature.
University of Illinois, 1965. 208 pages. Order 65-11,797.

   Melville's confidence men aboard the Fidèle follow the tradition of
   mythic figures perennially assaulting innocent victims, who are
   themselves the descendents of the American Adam. (DA: 26-2753)

139. Kenny, Vincent S. Herman Melville's Clarel. New York University,
1965. 297 pages. Order 66-5672.

   Given Clarel's aesthetics and themes of Titanism, despair and with-
   drawal, rejection, and resignation and acceptance; the poem serves as
   a summation of Melville's philosophy. (DA: 27-458)

   See: Kenny, Vincent S. "Clarel's Rejection of the Titans," American
   Transcendental Quarterly, 7 (Summer 1970), 76-81. Herman Melville's
   Clarel: A Spiritual Autobiography. Hamden, Ct.: Archon, 1973.

140. Long, Raymond Ronald. The Hidden Sun: A Study of the Influence of
Shakespeare on the Creative Imagination of Herman Melville. University of
California at Los Angeles, 1965. 340 pages. Order 65-13,857.

   With special attention to Ahab and Pierre, the study examines all of
   Melville's works for direct and indirect quotations of Shakespeare,
   characters patterned after the bard's incidents derived from his
   plays, similar syntactic constructions, phraseology, and connotations.
   (DA: 26-4634)

141. Pops, Martin Leonard. The Winding Quest: A Study of Herman
Melville. Columbia University, 1965. 402 pages. Order 68-5657. (DA:
28-4141)

   See: Pops, Martin Leonard. The Melville Archetype. Kent, Ohio:
   Kent State University Press, 1970.

142. Rosen, Bruce John. Typee and Omoo: Melville's Literary Apprentice-
ship. New York University, 1965. 304 pages. Order 66-5697.

   Separate chapters deal with the backgrounds, themes, structures,
   motifs, and styles of T and O. (DA: 27-461)

143. Semmens, John Edward. Point of View in the Early and Later Fiction
of Herman Melville. University of Notre Dame, 1965. 417 pages. Order
65-8504.

   Melville shifts his use of point of view, late and soon. In the social
   criticism of the early adventure narratives, he aligns himself with the
   defiant rebel, but from "Bartleby" on, the author becomes increasingly
   disengaged. (DA: 26-1028)

144. Silberman, Donald Joseph. Form and Point of View in Melville's
Fiction. SUNY-Buffalo, 1965. 404 pages. Order 65-10,173.

Melville's first-person works join documentary to Bildungsroman and
produce a view that is both reliable and unreliable. One chapter
traces the cause of the critical controversy over the meaning of BB
to its equivocating style. (DA: 27-187)

145. Trimpi, Helen Pinkerton. Romance Structure and Melville's Use of
Demonology and Witchcraft in Moby-Dick. Harvard University, 1965. 299
pages.

Melville's understanding of romance derives from Scott. Also important
are the notions of the superstitious hero and narrator which can be
traced to some forty-two aspects of witchcraft and demonology. Seen
in this context, MD is a romance that depends upon witchcraft and
demonology for its system of ideas.

See: Trimpi, Helen P. "Demonology and Witchcraft in Moby-Dick,"
Journal of the History of Ideas, 30 (October-December 1969), 543-62.
"Conventions of Narrative Romance in Moby-Dick," Southern Review, n.s.
7 (January 1971), 115-29.

146. Williams, John Brindley. The Impact of Transcendentalism on the
Novels of Herman Melville. University of Southern California, 1965. 269
pages. Order 65-8927.

Discussions of M, R, WJ, and MD point out that Melville shows an
interest in Emersonian self-reliance, particularly as an artistic
creed respecting the symbolic correspondences between nature and the
mind. (DA: 26-1052)

147. Zipes, Jack David. Studies of the Romantic Hero in German and
American Literature. Columbia University, 1965. 183 pages. Order
66-4781.

The paradoxical narrative structures of Heinrich von Kleist's Michael
Kohlaas and MD relate to the contradictory personalities of their
heroes. HM: 70-95. (DA: 27-191)

1966

148. Bach, Bert Coates. Narrative Point of View in the Fiction of Herman
Melville after Moby-Dick. New York University, 1966. 305 pages. Order
67-581.

Melville's narrative devices are points of departure for rhetorical
interpretations of P, the tales, IP, CM, and BB. (DA: 27-2494)

See: Bach, Bert C. "Melville's Israel Potter: A Revaluation of Its
Reputation and Meaning," Cithara, 7 (November 1967), 39-50.
"Melville's Theatrical Mask: The Role of Narrative Perspective in
his Short Fiction," Studies in the Literary Imagination, 2 (April,
1969), 43-55. "Melville's The Confidence-Man: Allegory, Satire, and

the Irony of Intent," <u>Cithara</u>, 8 (May 1969), 28-36. "Narrative
Technique and Structure in <u>Pierre</u>," <u>American Transcendental Quarterly</u>,
7 (Summer 1970), 5-8.

149. Bagley, Carol Lenore. <u>Melville's Trilogy: Symbolic Precursor of
Freudian Personality Structure in the History of Ideas</u>. Washington State
University, 1966. 334 pages. Order 66-13,549.

When taken together, <u>M</u>, <u>MD</u>, and <u>P</u> illustrate the playing out of the
Oedipal conflict. (<u>DA</u>: 27-1778)

150. Davis, Frank Mark. <u>Herman Melville and the Nineteenth-Century Church
Community</u>. Duke University, 1966. 337 pages. Order 67-6100.

This study deals with the religious community of Melville's youth,
his reactions to missionaries in the South Seas, and the role of the
church and churchmen in his writings. (<u>DA</u>: 27-3866)

151. Dew, Marjorie Cannon. <u>Herman Melville's Existential View of the
Universe: Essays in Phenomenological Interpretation</u>. Kent State
University, 1966. 277 pages. Order 67-9417.

Building from leading existential writers, the study examines
Melville's views in <u>M</u>, <u>P</u>, "Bartleby," "Benito Cereno," <u>Clarel</u>, and <u>BB</u>.
(<u>DA</u>: 28-672)

See: Dew, Marjorie. "The Attorney and the Scrivener: Quoth the
Raven, Nevermore," in <u>Bartleby the Scrivener: A Symposium</u>, ed. Howard
P. Vincent (Kent, Ohio: Kent State University Press, 1966), 94-103.
"The Prudent Captain Vere," <u>American Transcendental Quarterly</u>, 7
(Summer 1970), 81-85.

152. Fine, Ronald Edward. <u>Melville and the Rhetoric of Psychological
Fiction</u>. University of Rochester, 1966. 468 pages. Order 66-10,804.

This topical arrangement deals mainly with Melville's technique of
characterization and concludes that the author believed human action
and identity to be rhetorically grounded. (<u>DA</u>: 27-1364)

153. Graves, Robert Dorset. <u>Polarity in the Shorter Fiction of Herman
Melville</u>. Duke University, 1966. 175 pages. Order 66-12,730.

Melville's apparent awareness of opposites as interdependent,
alternatingly conflictive and harmonious discredits any description
of him as Manichean. (<u>DA</u>: 27-1821)

154. Halliburton, David Garland. <u>The Grotesque in American Literature:
Poe, Hawthorne, and Melville</u>. University of California at Riverside, 1966.
255 pages. Order 67-5850.

A phenomenological interpretation of Melville's use of the grotesque.
HM: 143-235. (<u>DA</u>: 27-3840)

155. Hutchinson, William Henry. <u>Demonology in Melville's Vocabulary of
Evil</u>. Northwestern University, 1966. 388 pages. Order 66-13,998.

The study isolates dominant images of evil in single words and traces those words through Melville's writings. The words appear in an appendix. (DA: 27-2132)

156. Key, James Albert. An Introduction to Melville's Bird Imagery.
Tulane University, 1966. 157 pages. Order 66-10,763.

Bird images nestle in T, O, and M. An appendix shows the frequency and location of birds in all of Melville's works. (DA: 27-1369)

See: Key, J. A. "Typee: A Bird's Eye View." Publication of the Arkansas Philosophical Association, 1: 28-36.

157. Tick, Stanley. Forms of the Novel in the Nineteenth Century:
Studies in Dickens, Melville, and George Eliot. University of California at San Diego, 1966. 253 pages. Order 66-11,250.

In P, Melville uses the symbolic romance in its most complex form.
HM: 104-62. (DA: 27-1349)

158. Zirker, Priscilla Allen. The Major and Minor Themes of Melville's
White-Jacket. Cornell University, 1966. 460 pages. Order 66-11,063.

A background analysis of the man-of-war narrative precedes sections on egalitarianism (major theme) and hatred of war (minor). Melville's arguments on flogging are explored in their historical and ideological settings. (DA: 27-1799)

See: Zirker, Priscilla Allen. "Evidence of the Slavery Dilemma in White-Jacket," American Quarterly, 18 (Fall 1966), 477-92.

1967

159. Archer, Lewis Franklin. Coleridge's Definition of the Poet and the
Works of Herman Melville and William Faulkner. Drew University, 1967. 478 pages. Order 67-14,370.

Coleridge's theory of the imagination allows us to see Melville as a prophet seeking a new kind of innocence which accepts extremes of light and dark, and as one who creates symbols to reconcile, or attempt to reconcile, extremes. HM: 105-260. (DA: 28-1810)

160. Boudreau, Gordon Vincent. Herman Melville: Master Mason of the
Gothic. Indiana University, 1967. 320 pages. Order 68-2266.

The Gothic includes not only the literary tradition but also eighteenth-century neo-Gothic manorial architecture, medieval ecclesiastical architecture, and freemasonry. The symbology of the cathedral and its constituent symbols (light and rock) are found throughout the works. (DA: 28-5007)

See: Boudreau, G.V. "Of Pale Ushers and Gothic Piles: Melville's Architectural Symbology," Emerson Society Quarterly, 18 (II Q 1972), 67-82.

161. Braun, Julie Ann. <u>Melville's Use of Carlyle's</u> <u>Sartor Resartus</u>:
1846-1857. University of California at Los Angeles, 1967. 242 pages.
Order 68-7457.

>   <u>Sartor Resartus</u> affected Melville's style, literary technique, ideas,
>   and characterizations, especially in <u>MD</u> and <u>P</u>. After <u>P</u> Melville's
>   interest in the work declined. (<u>DA</u>: 28-4622)

162. Eddy, Darlene Fern Mathis. <u>A Dark Similitude: Melville and the</u>
<u>Elizabethan-Jacobean Perspective</u>. Rutgers University, 1967. 443 pages.
Order 67-9245.

>   Melville read in the literature of the sixteenth and seventeenth
>   centuries. His markings of Shakespeare and Beaumont and Fletcher
>   indicate similar interests, and evidence of his affinities with the
>   early dramatists appears in <u>MD</u>, <u>P</u>, and <u>CM</u>. (<u>DA</u>: 28-626)

>   See: Eddy, D. Mathis. "Melville's Response to Beaumont and Fletcher:
>   A New Source for <u>The Encantadas</u>," <u>American Literature</u>, 40 (November
>   1968), 374-80. "Melville's Sicilian Moralist," <u>English Language Notes</u>,
>   8 (1971), 191-200. "Bloody Battles and High Tragedies: Melville and
>   the Theatre of the 1840's," <u>Ball State University Forum</u>, 13 (Winter
>   1972), 34-45.

163. Faigelman, Steven Henry. <u>The Development of Narrative Consciousness</u>
<u>in Moby-Dick</u>. Cornell University, 1967. 269 pages. Order 67-13,912.

>   Melville's philosophical skepticism relates to the manner in which he
>   employs Ishmael as narrator. Central here is the "Try-Works" chapter
>   and its conceit of the Catskill eagle. (<u>DA</u>: 28-2243)

164. Hoeffer, Jacqueline Stanhope. <u>After Moby-Dick: A Study of</u>
<u>Melville's Later Novels</u>. Washington University, 1967. 237 pages. Order
67-17,186.

>   In light of Christian symbolism, the major characters of the latter
>   novels represent Melville's attitude towards the human condition in
>   its most extreme forms. (<u>DA</u>: 28-2647)

165. Martineau, Stephen Francis. <u>Opposition and Balance: A Character-</u>
<u>istic of Structure in Hawthorne, Melville, and James</u>. Columbia University,
1967. 193 pages. Order 67-12,268.

>   A detailed analysis of <u>CM</u> reveals Melville's change of style after <u>MD</u>.
>   <u>BB</u> is a natural extension of the structure of <u>CM</u>. HM: 64-107. (<u>DA</u>:
>   28-1441)

166. Noel, Daniel Calhoun. <u>The Portent Unwound: Religious and</u>
<u>Psychological Development in the Imagery of Herman Melville, 1819-1851</u>.
Drew University, 1967. 512 pages. Order 67-14,378.

>   This study of spiral, linear, and circular imagery relies heavily
>   upon primary source materials and biographical and historical
>   scholarship. (<u>DA</u>: 28-1791)

>   See: Noel, Daniel C. "Figures in Transfigurations: <u>Moby-Dick</u> as
>   Radical Theology," <u>Cross Currents</u> (Spring 1970), 201-20.

167. Ryan, Robert Charles. Weeds and Wildings Chiefly: With a Rose or Two by Herman Melville. Reading Text and Genetic Text, edited from the Manuscripts, with Introduction and Notes. Northwestern University, 1967. 313 pages. Order 67-15,332.

> The reading text presents what Melville's final wording and ordering would have been had a fair copy been made without further revision. Notes identify allusions, possible sources, and critical commentary. The genetic text, a verbatim transcript (in interpreted form) of the surviving manuscript leaves, follows Melville's revisions through to his final version. This is accompanied by an analysis of the manu- scripts. A revised version of the thesis will appear in volume 13 of the Northwestern-Newberry edition of The Writings of Herman Melville. (DA: 28-2262)

168. Stevens, Sister Mary Dominic, O.P. Melville: Sceptic. Loyola University of Chicago, 1967. 291 pages.

> In light of the sceptics who influenced him, Melville's scepticism is basically an epistemological problem. His imagery illuminates his scepticism.

> See: Stevens, Aretta J. "The Edition of Montaigne: Read by Melville," Papers of the Bibliographical Society of America, 62 (I Q 1968), 130-34.

169. Tompkins, Jane Parry. Studies in Melville's Prose Style. Yale University, 1967. 328 pages. Order 67-8425.

> A group of adjectives recurring throughout T, M, and MD is the focus of this interpretive analysis of Melville's diction and syntax. (DA: 28-246)

170. Wadlington, Warwick Paul. The Theme of the Confidence Game in Certain Major American Writers. Tulane University, 1967. 268 pages. Order 68-4074.

> Melville's rhetorical use of the confidence game in MD, "Benito Cereno," and CM is studied beside works by Twain and Nathanael West. HM: 52-109. (DA: 28-3691)

> See: Wadlington, Warwick. "Ishmael's Godly Gamesomeness: Self Taste and Rhetoric in Moby-Dick," English Literary History, 39 (1972), 309-31. The Confidence Game in American Literature. Princeton, N.J.: Princeton University Press, 1975.

171. Werge, Thomas Alan. The Persistence of Adam: Puritan Concerns and Conflicts in Melville and Mark Twain. Cornell University, 1967. 211 pages. Order 68-3520.

> The Augustinian or Puritan conception of original sin as a corruption of nature figures prominently in MD. HM: 75-125. (DA: 28-3653)

> See: Werge, Thomas. "Moby-Dick and the Calvinist Tradition," Studies in the Novel, 1 (Winter 1969), 484-506.

1968

172. Bergstrom, Robert F. The Impulsive Counterchange: The Development and Artistic Expression of Melville's Religious Thought, 1846-1857. Duke University, 1968. 314 pages. Order 69-11,939. (DA: 30-272)

173. Boggs, John Campbell, Jr. Modern Egotism and Melville's Imagery: Effects of a Naturalistic Perspective on Symbolic Relationships in the Prose Fiction of Herman Melville. Columbia University, 1968. 368 pages. Order 71-17,569.

Melville's works reflect "a modern sensibility conditioned by the collapse of traditional structures of value." (DA: 32-421)

174. Cannon, Agnes Dicken. Melville's Concepts of the Poet and Poetry. University of Pennsylvania, 1968. 300 pages. Order 69-72.

In defining Melville's concept of the poet and the poet's function, the study argues that Melville chose irregular meters and rhymes deliberately to express his masculine subject matter. The most important stylistic influence on Clarel was Melville's rediscovery of Homer in 1860 and his reading of Arnold's "On Translating Homer" in 1869 or 1871. (DA: 29-2207)

See: Cannon, Agnes Dicken. "Melville's Use of Sea Ballads and Songs," Western Folklore, 23 (January 1964), 1-16. "On Dating the Composition of Clarel," Melville Society Extracts, 13 (January 1973), 6. "Melville's Concepts of the Poet and Poetry," Arizona Quarterly, 31 (Winter 1975), 315-38.

175. Corey, James Robert. Herman Melville and the Theory of Evolution. Washington State University, 1968. 104 pages. Order 69-3737.

Seen in the light of certain major works on evolution, MD views nature as both an Edenic Paradise and a place of life-and-death struggle. (DA: 29-3093)

176. Devers, James. Melancholy, Myth, and Symbol in Melville's "Benito Cereno": An Interpretive Study. University of California at Los Angeles, 1968. 304 pages. Order 69-1124.

"Benito Cereno" demonstrates the underlying malaise that led to the American Civil War. Cereno is a melancholiac à la Burton, and Delano is a Father-archetype unsuccessfully seeking atonement with the Son. (DA: 29-2671)

177. Goforth, David Slate. Melville's Shorter Poems: The Substance and the Significance. Indiana University, 1968. 339 pages. Order 69-4748.

Melville's choice of rhyme and stanza forms was unfortunate, but the range of subject matter and depth of treatment may have required the restrictions of traditional meter and form. Aspects of the fiction also related to the poetry. (DA: 29-3097)

36   Bibliography

178. Heitner, John Adrian. <u>Melville's Tragic Triad: A Study of his Tragic Visions</u>. University of Rochester, 1968. 316 pages. Order 68-9375.

The triad (as found in <u>MD</u> and <u>BB</u>) consists of a protagonist, antagonist, and figure of resolution. Melville's tragic visions are religious and ironic. (<u>DA</u>: 29-229)

179. Kerr, Howard Hastings. <u>Spiritualism in American Literature, 1851-1886</u>. University of California at Los Angeles, 1968. 279 pages. Order 69-5323.

Melville equates the Spiritualist movement, especially the Fox Sisters' rappings, with New England witchcraft in "The Apple-Tree Table." HM: 43-52. (<u>DA</u>: 29-3101)

180. McQuitty, Robert Alan. <u>A Rhetorical Approach to Melville's "Bartleby," "Benito Cereno," and Billy Budd</u>. Syracuse University, 1968. 179 pages. Order 69-8636.

This rhetorical analysis (à la Booth) argues for a moral, intellectual, and emotional interpretation of the texts with respect to three formal relationships: the narrator and reader, the narrator and his characters, the implied author and the narrator and his tale. (<u>DA</u>: 29-4010)

181. Meyn, Rolf. <u>"American Experience" in the Works of Herman Melville: Studies in Modern American Literary Criticism</u>. Hamburg University, 1968. 157 pages. (German).

Examining the arguments by which critics have classified <u>MD</u> as an American classic leads us to a better understanding of our definition of a "national literature." The frontier, folklore, democracy, puritanism, and the theme of innocence are crucial elements in the "American experience." The author doubts Melville's dependence upon folklore and does not feel that his works present a clear criticism of democratic society. (<u>EASG</u>, 1971, item 80)

182. Miller, Wayne Charles. <u>The American Military Novel: A Critical and Social History</u>. New York University. 1968.

See: Miller, Wayne Charles. <u>An Armed America--Its Face in Fiction: A History of the American Military Novel</u>. New York: New York University Press, 1970.

183. Nichols, Martha Frances. <u>Sun Imagery in the Novels of Herman Melville</u>. Tulane University, 1968. 110 pages. Order 68-15,255.

The sun is a motif in juxtaposition with the land; it figures in the theme of appearance and reality and serves as a religious and mythic symbol. The focus is <u>MD</u>. (<u>DA</u>: 29-1904)

184. Rysten, Felix Simon Anton. <u>False Prophets in Fiction: Camus, Dostoevsky, Melville, and Others</u>. University of Southern California, 1968. 272 pages. Order 69-6505

MD argues that man must unite, not in fear or in false hope, but in solidarity against one known reality: the indifference of the universe. HM: 168-212. (DA 29-3586)

See: Rysten, Felix S. A. False Prophets in the Fiction of Camus, Dostoevsky, Melville, and Others. Coral Gables, Fla: University of Miami Press, 1972.

185. Schmid, Mary Pauline. La poesie de la mer dans Victor Hugo et Herman Melville: Les Travailleurs de la mer et Moby-Dick. Toulouse, 1968. (DEAL, 1970)

186. Seltzer, Leon Francis. The Vision of Melville and Conrad: A Comparative Study. SUNY-Buffalo, 1968. 201 pages. Order 68-11,488.

Melville's and Conrad's similar world views led to their use of similar themes and techniques. Both are skeptical of man's egoistical motives; hence, both use ethically flawed characters and "doubles." Disenchanted with nature and the idea of a benevolent God, they both adopt an attitude of perpetual doubt or "ruminative non-commitment" and a concomitant ironic technique "designed to belie all routine formulas." As nihilists, the two compose open-ended works that invert traditional symbols and focus our attention on the narrator. Despite their nihilism, both feared a too-lucid exposure of their readers to reality's amoral structure; therefore they "speak in behalf" of illusory ideals that will nevertheless "nourish" man. (DA: 29-613)

See: Seltzer, Leon F. "Like Repels Like: The Case of Conrad's Antipathy for Melville," Conradiana 1 (Summer 1969), 101-5. The Vision of Melville and Conrad: A Comparative Study. Athens, Ohio: Ohio University Press, 1970.

187. Shurr, William Howard. The Symbolic Structure of Herman Melville's Clarel. University of North Carolina at Chapel Hill, 1968. 160 pages. Order 70-3316.

Clarel is one massive, complex and "very neatly constructed" symbol composed of three static elements: Jerusalem, the landscape, and the Dead Sea. Melville's consideration of various theories of history and his combining pastoral, edenic, and Christ material adds a more dynamic dimension to the symbol. (DA: 30-3477)

See: Shurr, William H. "Melville and Christianity." Essays in Arts and Sciences, 5: 129-48. The Mystery of Iniquity: Melville as Poet, 1857-1891. Lexington, Ky.: University Press of Kentucky, 1972.

188. Spininger, Dennis Joseph. Paradise and the Fall as Theme and Structure in Four Romantic Novels: Tieck's William Lovell, Chateaubriand's Atala and René, and Melville's Typee. University of Wisconsin, 1968. 385 pages. Order 69-999.

T portrays an unsuccessful quest, the protagonist of which symbolically and ironically re-enacts the fall, while aspiring to the new paradise. HM: 228-309. (DA: 29-4469)

1969

189. Bergmann, Johannes Dietrich. The Original Confidence-Man: The
Development of the American Confidence Man in the Sources and Backgrounds
of Herman Melville's The Confidence-Man: His Masquerade. University of
Connecticut, 1969. 245 pages. Order 69-12,722.

   Using contemporary newspaper accounts and writings, the study traces
   the development of the confidence man in America (especially New York)
   from 1835 to 1857 and determines how Melville drew upon this knowledge
   in CM. (DA: 30-678)

   See: Bergmann, Johannes D. "The Original Confidence Man," American
   Quarterly, 21 (Fall 1969), 560-77.

190. Bickley, Robert Bruce, Jr. Literary Influences and Technique in
Melville's Short Fiction: 1853-1856. Duke University, 1969. 295 pages.
Order 70-8016.

   The study locates Melville more precisely in the history and tradition
   of American short fiction, accounts for the literary influences upon his
   tales, and analyzes his craftsmanship and technique. (DA: 30-4935)

   See: Bickley, R. B. "The Minor Fiction of Hawthorne and Melville,"
   American Transcendental Quarterly 14 (Spring 1972), 149-52. "The
   Triple Thrust in Melville's Short Stories: Society, the Narrator, and
   the Reader." Studies in American Humor, 1 (January 1975), 172-9. The
   Method of Melville's Short Fiction. Durham, N.C.: Duke University
   Press, 1975.

191. Bray, Richard Thomas. Melville's Mardi: An Approach Through
Imagery. University of Wisconsin, 1969. 186 pages. Order 69-22,354.

   Four clusters of images dominate M: the romantic thrust (an attempt
   to reach a state of existence beyond normal reality), calms (man's
   sense of everlasting serenity), circles (man in the center of the
   cosmos), polarity (the duality of life). (DA: 30-5401)

192. Bredahl, Axel Carl, Jr. Melville's Angles of Vision: The Function
of Shifting Perspective in the Novels of Herman Melville. University of
Pittsburgh, 1969. 121 pages. Order 70-14,826.

   Melville's "psychological perspective," as opposed to narrative point
   of view, is crucial in exploring the implications of man's limitations.
   (DA: 31-1263)

   See: Bredahl, A. Carl, Jr., Melville's Angles of Vision. Gainesville,
   Fla.: University of Florida Press, 1972.

193. Brown, Margaret. Herman Melville and James Michener: American
Apostles of the Pacific. Tulane University, 1969.

194. Carothers, Robert Lee. Herman Melville and the Search for the
Father: An Interpretation of the Novels. Kent State University, 1969.
220 pages. Order 70-5953.

In Melville's novels, the Father (or creative principle and ultimate truth) is unknown to his children (or Ishmaelian castaways). In MD, to know the Father, or to catch glimpses of the truth, is to be driven mad or to be killed; to refuse the quest is to gain a new life. In BB, however, man without the Father must assume the role of world orderer, thus ending his life with the acceptance of necessity. (DA: 30-4445)

See: Carothers, Robert L. "Melville's 'Cenci': A Portrait of Pierre," Ball State University Forum, 10 (Winter 1969), 53-9.

195. Daiker, Donald Arthur. The Motif of the Quest in the Writings of Herman Melville. Indiana University, 1969. 284 pages. Order 70-7438.

From T to P, Melville's fiction focuses on the absolute quest. Beginning with PT, the quest for a limited goal replaces that of an absolute. Although Melville was convinced that neither quest could succeed, he nevertheless asserts its value by enlisting sympathy for the quester and by showing that the search itself leads to knowledge that would have otherwise not been obtained. (DA: 30-4979)

196. Doherty, Joseph Francis, Jr. The "Desolation of Solitude": Studies in American Solipsistic Loneliness During the First Half of the Nineteenth Century. University of Minnesota, 1969. 392 pages. Order 70-5558.

Melville's fiction manifests "the full force of isolation made inevitable by the modern metaphysics bequeathed to Western Man in the Cartesian model for defining existence." Although the author had no solution to the dilemma, he established it as a major theme for modern American literature. HM: 296-370. (DA: 30-4406)

197. Estrin, Mark Walter. Dramatizations of American Fiction: Hawthorne and Melville on Stage and Screen. New York University, 1969. 408 pages. Order 70-3060.

In discussing MD, "Benito Cereno," and BB, the study focuses on the problems of transforming rhetorical and narrative devices from fiction to drama and whether the distinction between romance and novel affects the transformation. HM: 214-382. (DA: 30-3428)

See: Estrin, M.W. "Robert Lowell's 'Benito Cereno,'" Modern Drama, 15 (1973), 411-25.

198. Franks, Jesse Gibson. Air and Brass: Faith, Philosophy, and Events in the First Six Novels of Herman Melville. Ball State University, 1969. 149 pages. Order 69-19,421.

This search into the prevailing nature of Melville's commentary on his times argues that the author's quest for spiritual peace involves an integration of his personality and concludes that the acceptance of the will of an inscrutable God is the only solution to any problem, humanly solvable or not. (DA: 30-2482)

199. Gerlach, John Charles. The Kingdom of God and Nineteenth Century American Fiction. Arizona State University, 1969. 439 pages. Order 69-16,478.

"Kingdom of God" is any period in which man can stand in the grace of God and participate in the pattern of salvation through the Messiah. Melville's novels, except MD, are his ironic expression of this theme. HM: 121-98. (DA: 30-1524)

See: Gerlach, John. "Messianic Nationalism in the Early Works of Herman Melville." Arizona Quarterly, 28 (Spring 1972), 5-26.

200. Grejda, Edward S. The Common Continent of Men: The Non-White Characters in the Fiction of Herman Melville. University of Pittsburgh, 1969. 165 pages. Order 69-17,486.

Non-white characters relate to plot, theme, attitudes of and treatment by whites, Melville's imagery and editorial commentary, and physical and moral qualities. (DA: 30-1566)

See: Grejda, Edward S. The Common Continent of Men: Racial Equality in the Writings of Herman Melville. Port Washington, N.Y.: Kennikat, 1974.

201. Harold, Charles Brent. The Theme of Artistic Transformation in the Novel. Stanford University, 1969. 244 pages. Order 69-13,961.

MD and "Bartleby" record the frustrations of verbally aggressive men in imposing their visions on the environment. CM is an unsatisfying drama of the sophisticated artificer modeling himself on Mother Nature. HM: 42-60, 152-55. (DA: 30-1135)

202. Herbert, Thomas Walter, Jr. Spiritual Exploration in Moby-Dick: A Study of Theological Background. Princeton University, 1969. 313 pages. Order 70-14,252.

Melville rejected his early exposure to Dutch Reformed Calvinism and Unitarian liberalism. MD is his statement that the Power behind all mortal events must either be malignant or wantonly indifferent to man's plight. (DA: 31-1278)

See: Herbert, T. Walter, Jr. "Calvinism and Cosmic Evil in Moby-Dick," PMLA, 84 (October 1969), 1613-19. Moby-Dick and Calvinism: A World Dismantled. New Brunswick, N.J.: Rutgers University Press, 1976.

203. Hill, Douglas Baldwin, Jr. Studies in the Development of First-Person Narrative in American Literature to 1850. Columbia University, 1969. 196 pages. Order 70-6996.

Formal connections exist between MD and Melville's earlier first-person
narratives. HM: 102-16, 129-32. (DA: 30-4414)

204. Hoover, Walter Bruce. Aesthetic-Ethical Duplicity in Melville. University of Alberta, 1969. 341 pages.

Melville belongs to the Christian existentialist tradition of Kierkegaard, Berdyaev, and Unamuno.

205. Kirkland, James Wilton. Animal Imagery in the Fiction of Herman Melville. University of Tennessee, 1969. 231 pages. Order 70-17,828.

Melville uses animal imagery in his fiction to develop the themes of Primitivism versus civilization; initiation and self-discovery; head versus heart; the balance of nature and the American national character. (DA: 31-1803)

206. Klein, Yvonne Mathews. The Politics of the American Military Novel. University of Minnesota, 1969. 239 pages. Order 70-5640.

Military novels such as WJ explore the irony of democracy's dependence on an anti-democratic institution. HM: 10-28. (DA: 2388)

207. Kotzin, Miriam Naomi. Putnam's Monthly and Its Place in American Literature. New York University, 1969. 226 pages. Order 70-16,082.

This discussion of Melville's contributions to Putnam's poses the problem of whether the magazine's critical tenets affected his pieces. HM: 30-38, 205-6. (DA: 31-1232)

See: Kotzin, Miriam. "Putnam's Monthly and Herman Melville," Melville Society Extracts, 24 (1975): 4-5.

208. Lang, Wolfgang. Literary Short Prose Themes and Structure in Early American Magazines: A Contribution to the Theory of the American Short Story at the Time of Hawthorne and Poe. University of Tübingen, 1969. 305 pages. (German).

An exhaustive study of 800 fiction and non-fiction pieces drawn from seven important 19th century magazines yields a variety of structural deviations from classical tale form to numerous thematic categories. "The informal essay" and "moral treatise" have been excluded. Although Irving, Poe, and Hawthorne receive most of the attention, parallels between MD and BB and the sea adventure motif in early magazine fiction are drawn. (EASG, 1970, item 57)

209. Mandel, Ruth B. Herman Melville and the Gothic Outlook. University of Connecticut, 1969. 205 pages. Order 70-1288.

This study of Melville's familiarity and use of gothicism in MD, P, and "Benito Cereno" shows that Melville was a gothicist in the broader sense. (DA: 30-3015)

See: Mandel, R.B. "The Two Mystery Stories in 'Benito Cereno,'" Texas Studies in Literature and Language, 14 (Winter 1973), 631-53.

210. Middleton, John Alexander. Shark Talk: The Uses of Dialogue in Moby-Dick. Indiana University, 1969. 174 pages. Order 70-7481.

Melville's dialogue in MD reflects both the external world of action in the book and the interior workings of its characters. (DA: 30-4995)

211. Puett, Amy Elizabeth. Melville's Wife: A Study of Elizabeth Shaw Melville. Northwestern University, 1969. 323 pages. Order 70-141.

This study of Elizabeth Shaw's life before, during, and after her marriage to Melville provides a new perspective on that relationship and her impact on the author's life and work. Appended are Elizabeth's notes on her husband's life and a calendar of her letters. (<u>DA</u>: 30-2666)

212. Reed, Walter Logan. <u>Meditations of the Hero: Narrative Form in Carlyle, Kierkegaard, and Melville</u>. Yale University, 1969. 315 pages. Order 70-16,240.

Sartor Resartus, Fear and Trembling, and <u>MD</u> involve an intrusive narrator's meditations upon a central heroic figure. HM: 18-20, 209-80. (<u>DA</u>: 31-1288)

See: Reed, Walter L. <u>Meditations on the Hero: A Study of the Romantic Hero in Nineteenth-Century Fiction</u>. New Haven, Ct.: Yale University Press, 1974.

213. Reiss, John Peter, Jr. <u>Problems of the Family Novel: Cooper, Hawthorne, and Melville</u>. University of Wisconsin, 1969. 246 pages. Order 69-9714.

<u>P</u> is a "family novel," a subgenre of American fiction. Also discussed is the Cooper-Hawthorne-Melville relationship. HM: 94-140. (<u>DA</u>: 30-1178)

214. Schultz, Donald Deidrich. <u>Herman Melville and the Tradition of the Anatomy: A Study in Genre</u>. Vanderbilt University, 1969. 412 pages. Order 70-5463.

Melville's fiction bears a resemblance to the formal characteristics of the anatomy, also termed Menippean or Lucianic satire. The tension between the romance and the anatomy is a basic force in the author's writing. (<u>DA</u>: 30-4463)

215. Sommer, Gerd. <u>The First-Person Narrative in American Short Fiction of the 19th Century</u>. University of Erlangen-Nürnberg, 1969. 379 pages. (German).

A poetics of nineteenth-century short fiction involves three types of first-person narratives: <u>the factive</u> which explains the external world; <u>the impressive</u> in which the "I" confronts, influences, and is influenced by another individual; and <u>the expressive</u> in which speaker and external world coalesce. "Bartleby" falls under the "impressive" rubric. Also treated are Hawthorne, Poe, and James. (<u>EASG</u>, 1971, item 79)

216. Stencel, Michelle M. <u>Knowledge in the Novels of Herman Melville</u>. University of South Carolina, 1969. 285 pages. Order 70-9315.

Since man is limited to partial knowledge, he has four alternatives: cling to surface reality and ignore the unknown altogether; hide the implications of the unknown by substituting rigid doctrines; transmute hidden anxiety into a wrathful assault of the unknown; appreciate man's efforts to know and to accept the inability to know. (<u>DA</u>: 30-4956)

217. Turlish, Lewis Afton. <u>A Study of Teleological Concepts in the Novels</u>
<u>of Herman Melville</u>. University of Michigan, 1969. 102 pages. Order
70-4212.

Melville's acceptance of the teleological conception of the natural
order, as derived from Paley's <u>Natural Theology</u> and John Mason Good's
<u>The Book of Nature</u>, in his early novels gives way to a vacillation
between belief and disbelief in <u>M</u>. <u>MD</u> and <u>P</u> negate the teleological
premise, and <u>CM</u> reflects Melville's deprecation of "teleological
monism," a precursor of social Darwinism. (<u>DA</u>: 30-3922)

218. Watson, Charles Nelles, Jr. <u>Characters and Characterization in the</u>
<u>Works of Herman Melville</u>. Duke University, 1969. 256 pages. Order
70-11,597.

This investigation of the sources and influences, the techniques of
presentation, and the kinds of characters that Melville created
concludes that the author's inconsistent characters are true to life
and, like man, God, and the universe, remain inscrutable.
(<u>DA</u>: 31-372)

See: Watson, Charles N., Jr. "Melville's Agatha and Hunilla: A
Literary Reincarnation," <u>English Language Notes</u>, 6 (December 1971),
114-18. "Melville's Jackson: Redburn's Heroic 'Double,'" <u>Emerson</u>
<u>Society Quarterly</u>, 62 (Winter 1971), 8-10. "Melville and the Theme of
Timonism: From <u>Pierre</u> to <u>The Confidence Man</u>," <u>American Literature</u>, 44
(November 1972), 398-412.

219. Yellin, Jean Fagan. <u>The Negro in Pre-Civil War Literature</u>.
University of Illinois, 1969. 305 pages. Order 69-15,425.

"Benito Cereno" is an artistic statement as complex as Jefferson's
theoretical formulations in that it utilizes and destroys the stock
versions of the black presented in the earlier fiction. (<u>DA</u>: 30-1187)

See: Yellin, Jean F. "Black Masks: Melville's 'Benito Cereno,'"
<u>American Quarterly</u>, 22 (Fall 1970), 678-89. <u>The Intricate Knot: The</u>
<u>Negro in American Literature, 1776-1863</u>. New York: New York Univer-
sity Press, 1973.

1970

220. Amzalak, Yael. <u>Herman Melville en France: Attitude et reactions de</u>
<u>la critique française aux oeuvres de Melville depuis 1846</u>. University of
Paris, 1970. 145 pages.

221. Babin, James Lee. <u>Herman Melville and the Idea of Order</u>. Duke
University, 1970. 226 pages. Order 70-21,984.

"Order" is that state in which human existence and activity are
perceived as meaningful. Melville's writings represent his own

conflict in deciding between traditional (acceptance of temporality) and gnostic (relief from the tension of existence) conceptions of order. (<u>DA</u>: 31-2372)

See: Babin, James L. "Melville and the Deformation of Being from Typee to Leviathan," <u>Southern Review</u>, n.s. 7 (January 1971), 89-114.

222. Barbour, James Francis. <u>The Writing of Moby-Dick</u>. University of California at Los Angeles, 1970. 228 pages. Order 71-13,984.

Building from Howard's theory of two <u>MD</u>'s, this study proposes three stages of composition: romantic whaling tale, whaling facts, and dark quest for truth. (<u>DA</u>: 31-6538)

See: Barbour, James. "The Composition of <u>Moby-Dick</u>," <u>American Literature</u>, 48 (November 1975), 343-90. "'The Town-Ho's Story': Melville's Original Whale," <u>Emerson Society Quarterly</u>, 21 (IIQ 1975), 111-15. and Leon Howard. "Carlyle and the Conclusion of <u>Moby-Dick</u>," <u>New England Quarterly</u>, 49: 212-24.

223. Branch, Watson Gailey, <u>The Confidence-Man: His Masquerade, by Herman Melville. An Edition with an Introduction and Notes</u>. Northwestern University, 1970. 605 pages. Order 71-1804.

Parts of this critical edition of <u>CM</u> (including reproductions of Manuscripts) will appear in volume 10 of the Northwestern-Newberry edition of <u>The Writings of Herman Melville</u>. (<u>DA</u>: 31-3496)

See: Branch, Watson G. "The Genesis, Composition, and Structure of <u>The Confidence-Man</u>," <u>Nineteenth-Century Fiction</u>, 27 (1973), 424-48.

224. Cannon, Margaret Hart. <u>The Sole Survivor: A Romantic Motif</u>. University of North Carolina at Chapel Hill, 1970. 279 pages. Order 71-11,680.

An important "motif" in American fiction is that of "the <u>isolato</u> who alone survives the wreck of ship and crew and returns ... to tell his story...." Ishmael is discussed. HM: 91-136. (<u>DA</u>: 31-6004)

225. Christy, Wallace McVay. <u>The Shock of Recognition: A Psycho-Literary Study of Hawthorne's Influence on Melville's Short Fiction</u>. Brown University, 1970. 157 pages. Order 71-13,845.

As Melville "was entering the most creative, and destructive, period of his psychic life," Hawthorne reinforced his need to love another man and influenced many technical aspects of Melville's short fiction. (<u>DA</u>: 31-6543)

226. Farwell, Harold Frederick, Jr. <u>The Relation of Point of View and Style in Four Early Novels of Herman Melville</u>. University of Wisconsin, 1970. 467 pages. Order 70-20,837.

Melville's characters in <u>T</u>, <u>O</u>, <u>M</u>, and <u>MD</u> project the author's basic desires. (<u>DA</u>: 31-2912)

227. Flibbert, Joseph Thomas. Melville and the Art of Burlesque.
University of Illinois at Champaign, 1970. 252 pages. 71-14,744.

Melville adopted literary fashions of his time, but almost always with
some sense of irony. Skepticism and humor unite in CM. (DA: 31-6602)

See: Flibbert, Joseph. Melville and the Art of Burlesque.
Amsterdam: Rodopi, 1974.

228. Freibert, Sister Lucy Marie. Meditative Voice in the Poetry of
Herman Melville. University of Wisconsin, 1970. 410 pages. Order
70-20,839.

This rhetorical analysis of the poetry argues that the meditative
voice, which combines the elegiac strain of the literary tradition and
the techniques of formal meditation, is the distinguishing characteristic of Melville's work. The poems reflect the author's reading of
English and Continental poets, including Elizabeth Barrett Browning,
Camoens, and La Fontaine. (DA: 31-2875)

229. Henchey, Richard Francis. Herman Melville's Israel Potter: A Study
in Survival. University of Massachussetts, 1970. 194 pages. Order
70-17,989.

The central theme of survival in IP is displayed in four modes:
reason (Franklin), impulse (Jones), freedom (Allen), and role-playing
(Potter). (DA: 31-1758)

230. Lape, Denis Allison. "The Masks of Dionysus": An Application of
Friedrich Nietzsche's Theory of Tragedy to the Works of Hawthorne and
Melville. University of Minnesota, 1970. 305 pages. Order 71-18,866.

The deepest tragedies of Hawthorne and Melville are "Dionysian,"
focusing on a tragic hero who "redeems the spectator from the
'nausea' induced by the tragic vision." Though often mad or criminal,
the heroes are beyond good or evil, suffering from excesses rather
than deficiencies of power and vitality. Their struggle restores to
us a sense of unity and value. Melville's discovery of Hawthorne
inspired "his supreme Dionysian tragedy, MD." Ahab embodies the
redemptive power of Dionysian tragedy: "His fate restores our faith
in the power of life, and expresses Melville's titanic rebellion
against his culture." In the later works, Melville moves from a
dynamic affirmation to a static negation, from tragedy to naturalism.
(DA: 32-5188)

231. Lester, James D. Melville's The Piazza Tales: The Quest for
Communication. University of Tulsa, 1970. 137 pages. Order 71-13,531.

Three barriers create communication breakdowns among men: distortions
due to social norms, the closed mind of self-centered man, and the
misreading of signs and symbols. (DA: 31-6015).

232. Martineau, Barbara Joan. Dramatized Narration in the Short Fiction
of Irving, Poe, and Melville. Columbia University, 1970. 205 pages.
Order 71-6223.

Melville's storytelling technique develops from a traditional use of point of view in "The Town-Ho's Story" to CM where there is "little possibility of understanding among narrator, audience, and reader." HM: 122-88. (DA: 31-4725)

233. Moore, Dennis James. The Transformations of Billy Budd: The Making of a Modern Myth. Northwestern University, 1970. 218 pages. Order 71-10,165.

BB is a modern myth echoed in Trilling's Middle of the Journey, Wouk's The Caine Mutiny, and Lowry's Lunar Caustic. Dramatizations of the tale by Coxe and Chapman (play), Ustinov (film), and Britten (opera) present problems of interpretation and adaptation. (DA: 31-5417)

234. Paluska, Duane Alan. The Dead Letter Office: A Study of Melville's Fiction, 1852-1857, With a Checklist of Writings Related to Melville's Tales, Israel Potter, and The Confidence-Man. Brandeis University, 1970. 221 pages. Order 70-24,652.

"Mosses" is Melville's self-portrait as America's literary Messiah. After the public's refusal to confirm this, the author turned from heroic quest tale to stories of failure, retreat, and alienation. CM is "the culmination of a unique set of gradually solved literary problems." The Checklist is a selective, annotated coverage of twentieth-century criticism up to 1968. DA: 31-2934)

235. Sandberg, Alvin. The Quest for Love and the Quest for Revenge in Herman Melville. New York University, 1970. 245 pages. Order 71-15,427.

Melville's relationship with his parents and the "strong latent homo-sexual components" in his personality are themes which allow us "a comprehensive psychoanalytic interpretation" of the prose works. (DA: 31-6568)

See: Sandberg, Alvin. "Erotic Patterns in 'The Paradise of Bachelors and the Tartarus of Maids,'" Literature and Psychology, 8 (1968), 2-8.

235.5 Santraud, Jeanne-Marie. La mer et le roman américain dans la première moitié du 19e siècle. University of Paris, 1970. (DEAL, 1877)

See: Santraud, Jeanne-Marie. "La Signification du voyage pour les écrivains navigateurs américains de 1800 à 1851," in Le Voyage dans la littérature anglo-saxonne, ed. Sociète des Anglisticistes de l'Enseignement Superior. (Paris: Didier, 1972), 91-116. La Mer et le roman américain dans la première moitié du dix-neuvieme siècle. Paris: Didier, 1972.

236. Seltzer, Alvin Jay. Chaos in the Novel--The Novel in Chaos. Pennsylvania State University, 1970. 673 pages. Order 71-21,801.

MD and CM are chaotic novels because of the tension in them between "form and a vision which denies every assumption on which that form rests." HM: 59-110. (DA: 32-984)

237. Smith, Kenneth Daniel. Dramatic Adaptations of Herman Melville's Billy Budd. University of Notre Dame, 1970. 250 pages. Order 71-5559.

The eleven English language dramatizations of <u>BB</u> reveal disparate attitudes on the adaptors' parts with respect to "such issues as order, justice, law, morality, duty, and private conscience." Bibliography includes reviews, and published and manuscript adaptations. (<u>DA</u>: 31-4734)

238. Smith, Leverett Tyrell, Jr. <u>The American Dream and the National Game</u>. University of Minnesota, 1970. 533 pages. Order 71-8267.

Twentieth century man has shifted from a work to a play ethic. In some literary works, the world of professional sports presents "an ethic alternative to the supposed ethics of the commercial democratic society as a whole." Ahab, in some respects, resembles the public image of Vince Lombardi. HM: 388-400. (<u>DA</u>: 32-1530)

239. Wolfrum, Max Douglas. <u>Responsible Failure in Melville</u>. Washington University, 1970. 223 pages. Order 70-18,938.

Melville envisioned three levels of existence: the horological (what is), the chronometrical (what ought to be), and the expedient (the best that can be). After abandoning Nature, Christianity, and democracy as possible solutions to the problem of existence, Melville decided that the best available course was the resignation of Vere, "an unpalatable but unavoidable expediency." (<u>DA</u>: 31-1821)

1971-1980

1971

240. Bellis, George David. <u>Moby-Dick and a Philosophy of Will</u>. The
Catholic University of America, 1971. 156 pages. Order 71-25,552.

> The major "Force" in <u>MD</u> is Will, "best identified in an anthropomorphic
> sense with the God of the Gnostic tradition." Melville's novel is
> also discussed in the light of Schopenhauer. (<u>DA</u>: 32-2050)

241. Bridges, Lloyd. <u>Flight in the American Novel</u>. University of Utah,
1971. 181 pages. Order 72-496.

> Biblical, Greek and Roman traditions shape the "American flight
> narrative." <u>MD</u> is America's "ultimate flight" in which Ishmael, like
> Odysseus, seeks something that he has missed on shore, and Ahab
> searches for ultimate truth. HM: 25-38. (<u>DA</u>: 32-3243)

242. Bruner, Margaret Reed. <u>The Gospel According to Herman Melville: A
Reading of The Confidence-Man: His Masquerade</u>. Vanderbilt University,
1971. 355 pages. Order 72-15,468.

> Neither darkly pessimistic nor cynical, but rather tentative, <u>CM</u> is "a
> sympathetic exposition of essential Christianity." With references to
> Melville's use of the Bible, the study argues that the lamb-like Mute
> and Frank Goodman are Christ, one person in two disguises, and that a
> symbolic crucifixion occuring in Chapter one leads to a resurrection
> in Chapter 23. (<u>DA</u>: 32-6368)

243. Carlson, Constance Hedlin. <u>Heroines in Certain American Novels</u>.
Brown University, 1971. 198 pages. Order 72-8094.

> Heroines in the works of Wharton, Fitzgerald, and Updike are
> contrasted with the heroines of Cooper, Melville, Cather, and
> Hemingway. Melville sees American women as the purveyors of society's
> hypocrisies and strictures. Fayaway offers an escape from America's
> professed ideals. In <u>P</u> the feminine triangle of the hero's mother,
> Lucy, and Isabel is an incisive symbol of the castrating tendencies of
> American women. Melville's rage against the pressures which engulf
> and doom Pierre equals that of Hemingway. HM: 17-31. (<u>DA</u>: 32-5175)

244. Chaffee, Patricia Ann. The Lee Shore: Volition, Time, and Death in the Fiction of Herman Melville. Indiana University, 1971. 180 pages. Order 72-6757.

Tense polarities in Melville's fiction between determinism and free will, historical time and mythical time, and death and life lead not to resolutions but to continually shifting emphases which restate the problem of each dilemma. In its treatment of M, WJ, MD, P, "Bartleby," and BB, the study shows Melville moving toward a recognition that necessity dominates freedom. (DA: 32-4556)

See: Chaffee, Patricia. "Paradox in Melville," American Transcendental Quarterly, 29: 80-83.

245. Davis, John Wesley Ford. A Theory of the Novel: Its Generic Impulse and Controlling Principle. Stanford University, 1971. 240 pages. Order 71-19,670.

Calling MD a metaphysical novel, the study argues that the work derives its tension from "the conflict between the ideal and the real and thus achieves a poetry of realism." Melville is treated as a modern novelist "whose works exemplify ... seemingly radical deviational possibilities of the genre." HM: 180-197. (DA: 32,961)

246. Fendelman, Judith. A Study of the Anatomy as a Prose Form in Burton's Anatomy of Melancholy, Sterne's Tristram Shandy, and Melville's Moby-Dick. Yale University, 1971.

247. Haberstroh, Charles Joseph, Jr. Melville's Fathers: A Study of the Father Substitutes in Melville's Fiction. University of Pennsylvania, 1971. 327 pages. Order 72-6157.

In the earlier works, the father is seen as a noble savage, a beachcomber, a bride, and a glorified tar. For P and after, these strategies "collapse," but BB provides "reconciliation and forgiveness." (DA: 32-4564)

See: Haberstroh, Charles. "Redburn: The Psychological Pattern," Studies in American Fiction, 2 (Autumn 1974), 133-44. "Melville, Marriage, and Mardi," Studies in the Novel, 9 (1977): 247-60. Melville and Male Identity. Rutherford, N.H.: Farleigh Dickinson University Press, 1980; London: Associated Press, 1980.

248. Heckman, Sally Lentz. Moby-Dick and the Process of Understanding. Rutgers University, 1971. 183 pages. Order 72-831.

MD records the process of understanding: the attempt "to create coherence from the multiple signs in this panoramic world." Ishmael's explanations "cause us to think that meaning is a process and not a product." (DA: 32-3252)

249. Hughes, Charles W. Man Against Nature: Moby-Dick and "The Bear." Texas Technical University, 1971. 156 pages. Order 72-10,354.

MD and Faulkner's tale provide two stages of America's struggle against nature. Whereas Melville's whale represents a mid-19th century view of inexhaustible natural resources, the death of Old

Ben signals the destruction of nature in America. Hunters, their quarrels, and hunting rituals are examined. (DA: 32-5230)

250. Keith, Philip Myron. The Idea of Quakerism in American Literature. University of Pennsylvania, 1971. 290 pages. Order 72-17,376.

Quaker thought helped shape the developing tradition of American literature through Whitman. Melville uses Quaker material to develop complex, ambiguous attitudes towards transcendentalists and Puritans. Old and new Quaker sensibilities (spiritualism vs. industrialism) come together in MD, but Moredock's Indian Hating in CM opposes Quaker pacifism. HM: 142-79. (DA: 32-6933)

251. Lenson, David Rollar. Examples of Modern Tragedy. Princeton University, 1971. 244 pages. Order 72-13,746.

The impulse to write tragedy in the Romantic period shifted from theatre to other genres: the Nouvelle, the novel, and the lyric poem. Melville's use of Ishmael as a chorus in response to Ahab places the structure of MD at the foundations of tragedy. The study prefers the tragic theories of Hegel and Nietzsche to Aristotle's, defines the tragic hero as one who must choose between glory and longevity, and treats modern works by Kleist, Yeats, Faulkner, Giraudoux, and Becket. HM: 66-102. (DA: 32-6433)

252. Lish, Terrence G. Name Symbolism in Melville's Pierre and a Selective Onomastic Glossary for his Prose. University of Nevada, 1971. 135 pages. Order 72-2610.

Melville uses names to underscore superficial qualities (place, job, appearance, or personality), but his use of names for characterization and symbolism especially in the later works show greater subtlety. Name symbolism contributes much to the thematic coherence of Pierre, bringing together pagan, early Christian, and modern reflections on the action. Included is a list of names from Melville's prose fiction which have symbolic connotations. (DA: 32-4007)

253. Marshall, Donald Ray. The Green Promise: Greenness as a Dominant Symbol in the Quest for Eden in American Fiction. University of Connecticut, 1971. 450 pages. Order 71-18,428.

Irving, Cooper, and Poe explore the possibilities of Greenness as a symbol, but as the age became more, introspective, Hawthorne and Melville manifested far less concern with America's verdant landscape than the hazards of an internal greenness. T, MD, and P are discussed. HM: 85-113. (DA: 32-925)

254. May, John Richard. Apocalypse in the American Novel. Emory University, 1971. 201 pages. Order 72-3038.

The traditional apocalyptic pattern of judgment, catastrophe, and renewal derived from primitive and Judaeo-Christian sources appears in a large body of American writing, from Hawthorne to Pynchon. The definitive secular version of the loosed Satan appears in CM. Although Melville's imagination of doom is muted, he presents an apocalypse of despair and does not see a future worth living. (DA: 32-4009)

See: May, John R. <u>Toward a New Earth: Apocalypse in The American</u>
<u>Novel</u>. Notre Dame, Ind.: University of Notre Dame Press, 1972.

255. Melton, Willas Sayre. <u>An Assessment of the Position of Transforma-</u>
<u>tional-Generative Grammar in Stylistic Analysis</u>. University of Tulsa,
1971. 116 pages. Order 71-24,316.

Brief stylistic observations are made on the "quantitative variations
... in the sentences of the narrative and cetological sections" of
<u>MD</u>. HM: 82-91. (<u>DA</u>: 32-1482)

256. Metwalli, Ahmed Mohamed. <u>The Lure of the Levant</u>. <u>The American</u>
<u>Literary Experience in Egypt and the Holy Land: A Study in the Literature</u>
<u>of Travel, 1800-1965</u>. SUNY-Albany, 1971. 413 pages. Order 72-31,790.

Most prominent 19th century literary figures either wrote a travel
book of some kind or used their foreign travel in their work, but
travel literature as a genre remains unstudied. Briefly treated is
<u>Clarel</u> which succeeds as a quest for health but fails as a quest for
faith. HM: 353-9. (<u>DA</u>: 33-2899)

257. Nascimento, Daniel Cunha. <u>Melville's Berkshire World: The Pastoral</u>
<u>Influence upon his Life and Works</u>. University of Maryland, 1971. 328
pages. Order 72-10,083.

After <u>MD</u>, Melville's failure to please the reading public and his
movement from longer to shorter prose works and then to poetry
correspond to a shift in his view of the country. Originally an
idyllic pastoral setting, it became for him a scene of nature
perverted by industrial and social corruptions. Pastoral imagery in
<u>MD</u> provides a counterpoint to the ocean's savage nature. In <u>P</u>, the
Berkshire countryside is contrasted with a stark metropolitan
setting. The magazine pieces and <u>CM</u> reflect Melville's changing
attitude toward the Berkshire world. A new mood of a fallen rural
paradise appears. The trip to the Near East and the lecture tours
are attempts to escape from the Berkshire's pastoral environment.
(<u>DA</u>: 32-5193)

258. Schaible, Robert Manly. <u>An Annotated Edition of Herman Melville's</u>
<u>Redburn</u>. The University of Tennessee, 1971. 411 pages. Order 72-15,547.

Based on the Northwestern-Newberry text, this edition includes an
afterward reviewing the history of the book's composition and
publication, a survey of pertinent scholarship, a glossary of
nautical terms, a bibliography of editions, and notes explaining
references to art, literature, locations, monument, people and
Melville's life. (<u>DA</u>: 33-2343)

259. Short, Bryan Collier. <u>Herman Mellville's Poetry: The Growth of a</u>
<u>Post-Romantic Art</u>. Claremont Graduate School, 1971. 207 pages. Order
71-29,628.

Melville's career ends on a "note of achievement," as evidenced in
his technical innovations and movement away from romantic methods and
values. (<u>DA</u>: 32-2708)

See: Short, Bryan C. "'Betwixt the Chimes and Knell': Versification as Symbol in Clarel," Melville Society Extracts, 26:4. "Form as
Vision in Herman Melville's Clarel," American Literature, 50 (1977):
553-69. "'The Redness of the Rose': The Mardi Poems and Melville's
Artistic Compromise. Essays in Arts and Sciences, 5: 100-12.

260. Sten, Christopher Willie. The Necessary Angel of Herman Melville:
Studies in his Sense of an Ending. Indiana University, 1971. 102 pages.
Order 71-21,311.

A study of the endings of T, M, MD, "Bartleby," CM, and BB reveals
Melville's "recognition of the incompleteness of knowledge and the
consequent incompleteness of form." (DA: 32-934).

See: Sten, Christopher. "Bartleby the Transcendentalist: Melville's Dead Letter to Emerson," Modern Language Quarterly, 25 (March
1974), 30-44. "Vere's Use of the 'Forms': Means and Ends in Billy
Budd," American Literature, 47 (March 1975), 37-51.

261. Travis, Mildred Klein. Toward the Explication of Pierre: New Perspectives in Technique and Meaning. Arizona State University, 1971. 164
pages. Order 71-24,407.

Melville's art is examined from the perspectives of historical fact,
ambiguity, classical allusion and literary influence. (DA: 32-1534)

See: Travis, Mildred K. "Melville's 'Furies' Continued in Pierre,"
Emerson Society Quarterly, 62 (Winter 1971), 33-5. "Echoes of Emerson in Plinlimmon," American Transcendental Quarterly, 14 (Spring
1972), 47-8. "Relevant Digressions in Pierre," American Transcendental Quarterly, 24 (Fall 1974), 7-8.

262. Wells, John Francis. Herman Melville's Literary Reputation,
1940-1969. University of Minnesota, 1971. 217 pages. Order 71-28,321.

The three decades of criticism treated here fall into three
corresponding phases. Critics of the 1940's focused on Melville as a
social critic; the 1950's emphasized Melville's artistry as a
symbolist, and the 1960's turned to the author's narrative and
structural techniques and his existential learning. (DA: 32-2713)

263. Wolf, George Edward. Herman Melville's Experiments in Narration:
1852-1855. University of Connecticut, 1971. 228 pages. Order 71-29,927.

Lengthy discussions of "Bartleby," "The Encantadas," and BC, offer
proof that Melville's "artistry and deep concern for the writer's
craft" did not decline during the years immediately following MD.
(DA: 32-2658)

264. Wyss, Hal Huntington. Involuntary Evil in the Fiction of Brown,
Cooper, Poe, Hawthorne, and Melville. The Ohio State University, 1971.
257 pages. Order 71-22,552.

Like Hawthorne, Melville "concentrates on two kinds of evil, natural depravity and intellectual evil." Claggart is the best specimen of the former type to be found in American fiction, and Ahab represents a "culmination" of the latter type. HM: 199-249. (DA: 32-1489)

265. Young, Gloria L. The Sea as Symbol in the Work of Herman Melville and Joseph Conrad. Kent State University, 1971. 428 pages. Order 72-15,952.

Despite biographical similarities, parallel themes, and similar philosophical views, both authors used the sea differently. Melville's quest for meaning is idealistic and romantic, whereas Conrad's is realistic and existential. Discovering the absolute to be chartless, Melville ceases his voyaging. Conrad, on the other hand, recognizes that reason cannot comprehend the world, but he hopes the voyage itself will be of value. (DA: 32-6463)

1972

266. Axelrod, Steven Gould. Robert Lowell and American Literary Tradition. University of California at Los Angeles, 1972. 444 pages. Order 73-1681.

Melville is discussed in connection with "Benito Cereno," the major play of Lowell's The Old Glory trilogy. Unlike Melville's characters who play metaphysical roles, Lowell's are more political, historical, or psychological. In "revising" the work, Lowell is able to engage Melville in a dialog and to extend the meaning of his work. HM: 340-68. (DA: 33-4398)

267. Bird, Christine Murphy. Melville's Debt to Cooper's Sea Novels. Tulane University, 1972. 124 pages. Order 73-2184.

Melville's success in his sea novels derives from what he read, learned, and borrowed from the author of The Red Rover and The Sea Lions. Both writers mastered and improved on the conventional sea story, and like Cooper (according to Philbrick), Melville's early works developed from romance to realism to metaphysics. (DA: 33-4332)

See: Bird, Christine M. "Redburn and Afloat and Ashore," Nassau Review, 3, v: 5-16.

268. Brodhead, Richard Halleck. Polysensuum: Hawthorne, Melville, and the Form of the Novel. Yale University, 1972. 468 pages. Order 73-14,241.

MD and P, along with The Scarlet Letter and The House of the Seven Gables, form a unified phase in the history of the American novel. English novelists of the time created multiplicity by depicting a variety of overlapping lives. Melville's experiments with form attempt to achieve this effect not by telling several stories but by presenting several versions of one story. The mixed mode reflects "the ways in which the human imagination moves to give shape to and to make sense of its experience." HM: 229-398. (DA: 33-6863)

See: Brodhead, Richard H. Hawthorne, Melville, and the Novel.
Chicago: University of Chicago Press, 1976.

269. Burke, John Michael. A Bibliography of Soviet Russian Translations
of American Literature, 1948-1968. Brown University, 1972. 188 pages.
Order 73-2239.

Up until 1955, Soviet criticism of American literature followed
Marxist sociological criteria, and the works of Dreiser and Lewis
ranked highest. Since that time, views have liberalized, and the
acceptance of Melville in 1961 was an early manifestation of that
shift. (DA: 33-3576)

270. Carlson, Thomas Clark. 1. Melville's Fictive Voices before
Moby-Dick. 2. The Othello of Edwin Booth: a Reassessment. 3. The
Political Theme in Shakespeare's The Tempest. Rutgers University, 1972.
146 pages. Order 72-27,532.

In the five novels written before MD, Melville experiments with
various narrative masks in order to explore the dark and terrifying
nature of truth and, in part, to appease the reading public and John
Murray, who required objectivity in the supposed travelogs. HM:
1-70. (DA: 33-1675)

See: Carlson, Thomas C. "Fictive Voices in Melville's Reviews,
Letters, and Prefaces," Interpretations, 6 (1974): 39-46.

271. Combs, Barbara Sue. The Confidence-Man as Apocalyptic Vision. The
Ohio State University, 1972. 283 pages. Order 73-1971.

An anti-christ, representing the social, religious, and philosophical
views of his day, Melville's confidence man figure is agnostic, if
not nihilistic, and denies that any reality exists for the artist to
depict. With its patterns of role playing, disguise, and metamorphosis, the character develops as a theme related to the Quest from T to
IP. (DA: 33-4336)

272. Cook, Richard Merlyn. The Grotesque in the Fiction of Herman
Melville. The University of Michigan, 1972. 223 pages. Order 73-11,081.

According to Wolgang Kayser in The Grotesque in Art and Literature,
the grotesque is a traditional artistic medium for revealing contradiction and irrationality in the universe. Melville's use of the
grotesque also "dramatizes an irrevocable and often tragic
disjunction between human vision and final truth," which results in a
futile struggle to come to terms with the universe. (DA: 33-6304)

See: Cook, Richard M. "The Grotesque and Melville's Mardi," Emerson
Society Quarterly, 21 (IIQ 1975), 103-10. "Evolving the Inscrutable:
The Grotesque in Melville's Fiction," American Literature, 49:
544-59.

273. Curnow, Wystan Tremayne. <u>Melville's Poetry to 1876</u>. University of Pennsylvania, 1972. 215 pages. Order 72-25,559.

Just as Arnold turned to prose, Melville after confronting the problem of endurance in his later fiction, turned to poetry to secure a fresher vision. Whereas <u>BP</u> reveals Melville's inability to resolve philosophical and stylistic ambivalences, <u>Clarel</u> initiates a new phase of artistic development, that of the Aesthete. Through Vine and Rolfe, the long poem presents stylized ways of viewing the world. Style, then, is the work's primary feature, and as "a long Stylist poem," it is a success. (<u>DA</u>: 33-1719)

274. Daghlian, Carlos. <u>Persuasive Techniques in Moby-Dick</u>. University of São Paulo, 1972. 197 pages. (Portuguese).

Rhetorical influences on Melville and the scope of his rhetorical theory and practice are examined. Melville uses two rhetorical techniques. "Intra-rhetoric" involves one character (Mapple and Ahab) addressing other characters; "Extra-rhetoric" refers to Ishmael's address to the reader.

See: Daghlian, Carlos. "Alusões e Situações Retóricas em <u>Moby-Dick</u>," <u>Mimesis</u>, 2 (1976): 163-75.

275. Dehaven, Mary Alice. <u>The Fate of Innocence: Patterns of the Innocent's Encounter with the World of Nineteenth-Century English and American Fiction</u>. Case Western Reserve University, 1972. 241 pages. Order 72-18,681.

<u>BB</u> along with Crane's <u>Maggie</u> and Hardy's <u>Tess</u> portrays innocents who encounter evil persons yet reject themselves believing that society is right whereas their instincts are wrong. Of the three, Billy's innocence is purest, a presentation of an allegorical rather than realistic innocence. HM: 184-6. (<u>DA</u>: 32-6924)

276. Evans, Walter. <u>The Development of the Lyric Short Story in America, Irving to Melville</u>. The University of Chicago, 1972.

Critics recognize two main actions in short story form: the dynamic exterior action (developed by Irving, Poe, Hawthorne) and the internal or subjective action (characterized by lyricism begun by Turgenev). The origins of the lyric tradition, however, may be found in the essay-sketch heritage of Addison, Steele, and Irving. The bulk of Melville's short fiction resides "solidly in the essay-sketch tradition." Melville's debt to Hawthorne's sketches can be found in the author's finest lyric short fictions, "Bartleby" and "Benito Cereno." HM: 209-244.

277. Franklin, Wayne Steven. <u>Travelers Through Time: American Fiction and the American Travel Book, 1800-1860</u>. University of Pittsburgh, 1972. 300 pages. Order 72-22,315.

The 19th-century American novel is not primarily a romance but owes much to the travel book form. The American hero's voyaging leads him away from the familiar to an appalling newness. Lacking the fulfillment of the romance form, the traveler moves ever onward, into the new world of art, the ideal region of the mind. Along with Irving and Cooper, Melville is discussed extensively with respect to T, M, MD, IP, and CM. MD is also mentioned in a discussion of "Antiromance in American Travel Books and Don Quixote." HM: 206-53. (DA: 33-751)

278. Gamble, Richard Hugh. The Figure of the Protestant Clergyman in American Fiction. University of Pittsburgh, 1972. 238 pages. Order 73-1658.

In American literature, the clergyman is most often a romantic, exaggerated figure. An idealist, he struggles with the problem of living with absolute values in the actual world. Although Melville is not a primary focus here, attention is given to P. Pierre's attempt to live in a fallen world leads to violent discord and fragmentation. Plinlimmon provides an antiromantic voice, and the Rev. Mr. Falsgrave lies by his contrasting philosophy. HM: 48-51. (DA: 33-4343)

See: Gamble, Richard H. "Reflections on the Hawthorne-Melville Relationship in Pierre," American Literature, 47 (Spring 1975), 629-32.

279. Gulbenkian, Martha Vincent. A Study of Melville's Narrators from Typee to The Confidence-Man. Brandeis University, 1972. 197 pages. Order 73-15,446.

MD may be understood in the context of the "sailor-narrators" in the works which led up to and away from it. The early books are adventure tales told by individualized sailor-narrators which, when seen together, indicate a development toward Ishmael. After MD, the stature of the narrator declines. The later narrators are no longer sailors, are less fully realized, and reflect a negative viewpoint. The decline in the narrator correlates positively with the comparative weaknesses of the fiction after MD. (DA: 34-315)

280. Higgins, Brian. The English Background of Melville's Pierre. University of Southern California, 1972. 321 pages. Order 72-26,020.

Contemporary British works influenced Melville's conception and creation of P. Melville was trying to reach a select readership, but parallels between early sections of P and novels by Scott, Disraeli, and Bulwer-Lytton suggest that, at first, Melville was attempting a popular work. These irreconcilable intentions cause serious problems in Books I and II, and confusion for reviewers and critics. When Pierre moves to New York, the novel establishes a new impulse reminiscent of Dickens and Thackeray; but after Book XXI, Pierre is increasingly Byronized. Melville's objectivity and distance falters in his treatment of the young author attempting a mature work. An Appendix treats the meaning of Plinlimmon's pamphlet. (DA: 33-1726)

281. Hodgson, John Alfred. The World's Mysterious Doom: Melville and Shelley on the Failure of the Imagination. Yale University, 1972. 314 pages. Order 74-27,934.

Both Shelley and Melville were the paradigmatic skeptics of their
times, and each thinker developed in similar stages. Both move from
self-centered to selfless conceptions of Love (playing with or against
Plato), and both suffer the failure in the end of achieving
"imaginational fulfillment" in their work. Plato's "ladder of Love"
in Symposium serves as a measuring stick against which Pierre's
enthusiasm comes up short. Pierre's tragedy lies in his selfishness,
his inability to "sympathize." CM, too, borrows its form from Plato's
dialectic. It is through the novel's continual dialogues that
Melville is able to establish a vision that goes beyond Pierre's
futile storming. HM: 74-200; 245-99. (DA: 35-4431)

282. Kasson, Joy Schlesinger. Muses and Guidebooks: The Importance of
Tradition in American Literature and Painting, 1800-1860. Yale University,
1972. 325 pages. Order 73-14,564.

To examine the "impact of artistic tradition of the painting and
literature of the American Renaissance," the study shows how five
artists (Irving, Allston, Cooper, Cole and Hawthorne) attempted to
reconcile the opposing forces each felt toward European tradition and
New World subject matter. Melville and painter Frederic Church are
"pivotal" figures, illustrating the pre- and postcivil war genera-
tions. Both produced their best work before the War; both went beyond
the bounds of antebellum art. Melville's struggle is best seen in P
in which he "found that the development of an artistic form demanded
the synthesis of his own experience with the lessons learned from
artistic tradition." HM: 277-86. (DA: 34-322)

283. Kirk, Carey Harris. The Challenge of Involvement: A Response to
Melville and Conrad. Vanderbilt University, 1972. 173 pages. Order
72-26,111.

In their best known works, Melville and Conrad employ aesthetic techniques which aim to disorient, rather than communicate with, their
readers. This disorientation does not alienate readers, but it
challenges them, providing emotional and intellectual stimulation
instead of a more conventional conceptualized meaning. Four techniques
of reader engagement are examined here: open metaphors; changeable
characters or variable natural settings; attractive narrators; and
deceptively simple ethical or philosophical alternatives. (DA:
33-1731)

See: Kirk, Carey H. "Moby-Dick: The Challenge of Response," Papers
on Language and Literature, 13: 383-90.

284. Lorant, Laurie. Herman Melville and Race: Themes and Imagery. New
York University, 1972. 252 pages. Order 73-31,218.

Racial themes and imagery in Melville's writings are imaginative pro-
jections of the problems of slavery and reveal a broadminded attitude
well in advance of contemporary 19th century views. (DA: 34-3349)

285. Maier, Rosemarie Abendroth. Melville's Personae in Moby-Dick.
University of Illinois at Champaign, 1972. 314 pages. Order 73-9989.

Drawing upon Yeat's concept of the Mask and Jung's collective
unconsciousness, the author defines "persona" as a means by which
writers conceal and reveal aesthetic and psychic values. Frye's
notions of literary mode and genre are also applied in this
examination of the inconsistencies in MD. Ishmael's persona isolates
"young" and "elder" voices which commingle with other narrative and
non-narrative personae: the histor (providing digressive commentary),
the omniscient narrator (providing facts unknowable to Ishmael),
and three kinds of "anti-narrators" (which are not voices but which
"enhance the narrative quality of the art work"). These three are the
dramatist, the cetologist, and two "squitchy" voices (found in
"Etymology" and "Extracts"). (DA: 33-5685)

286. Mani, Lakshmi. The Apocalypse in Cooper, Hawthorne, and Melville.
McGill University (Canada), 1972.

The three featured artists used the apocalypse to criticize the pros-
perity, optimism, and spiritual myopia of their times. Melville makes
use of the Christian and Hindu archetypes and motifs to achieve a
vision of salvation. As does Hindu eschatology, Melville recognizes
evil as a principle of growth needed for the maturation of consciousness. Periodic dissolution of the universe dramatizes a fresh phase of
the cosmic struggle between good and evil. From the perspective of
this philosophy Melville was able to express his own Manichean concept
of evil. Treated works include MD, various tales, and CM. HM:
198-275.

287. Milder, Robert Warren. Herman Melville: A Prouder, Darker Faith.
Harvard University, 1972.

Two antagonistic impulses define the shape of Melville's tragic vision
whether in its rise or decline. The first, a profound humanitarianism,
begins with Melville's critique of the West in T and O, and culminates
in the "Ishmael Philosophy" of MD. The second, a predisposition toward
a nobler destiny than that afforded by "mere life," provides Melville
with the vision of transcendent heroism which informs Ahab but disinte-
grates in the later works because of Melville's penetration into the
human mind. Despite Melville's social sympathies, his deepest allegi-
ance was to the prouder, darker faith of his tragic heroes; and when
after MD, he ceased to believe in the psychological and metaphysical
possibility of tragedy, he was already on the path toward silence.
(Edited from author's abstract)

288. Montgomery, John Paul. The Creative Process and the Image of the
Artist in Melville's Mardi. Ohio University, 1972. 217 pages. Order
73-4241.

For Melville, M was an experimental novel, as well as a novel about
the process of creation itself. A review of criticism of the novel
reveals four questions: where is Melville in M? can a consistent
symbolic or allegorical reading of M be made: what do the five
questers represent? and what, if any, reading gives unity to M?
Answers are found by focusing on the artist in M. From the viewpoints
of the book's self-reflexive technique, M dramatizes symbolically the
artist at work both on his creation and on his own portrait. (DA:
33-4356)

289. Morgan, Sophia Steriades. Death of a Myth: A Reading of Moby-Dick
as Quixotic Literature. University of Michigan, 1972. 182 pages. Order
73-6882.

Quixotic literature is "marked by a conscious and manifest preoccupation with the problem of the relationship between books and reality,
or ... between reality and its representations." This central problem
in Don Quixote is also the main preoccupation of Ishmael and Ahab.
(DA: 33-5190)

290. Nelson, Gerald Lynn. Narrator as Character in Melville's Redburn.
University of Nebraska, 1972. 129 pages. Order 72-31,877.

Full appreciation of R comes with awareness of the unfolding of two
concurrent stories in the novel: the past tense story of the younger
Wellingborough, and the writing time story of the older Redburn
reflecting on his first voyage. In the former, the protagonist
evolves from idealism to realism; and, in the latter, the narrator
shifts from reporter to artist. Thus, the changing tone in the story
is not a flaw but a well-managed development. (DA: 33-2901)

291. Poenicke, Klaus. "Dark Sublime": Space and Self in American Romanticism. Jahrbuch fur Amerikastudien. Heidelberg: Carl Winter, 1972. 231
pages. (German).

The 19th century American conception of the sublime derives from Burke
and modifications of his thought provided by French revolutionaries.
Hawthorne and Melville, however, tend more toward the Kant-Schiller
re-evaluation of the "moral sublime." But Melville's principal heroes
(Taji, Ahab, Pierre) in their fanatical denials of nature only
"demonize" themselves and therefore parody the sublime. (EASG, 1972,
item 64)

292. Rosenzweig, Raul Jonathan. The Wilderness in American Fiction: A
Pscho-analytic Study of a Central American Myth. University of Michigan,
1972. 279 pages. Order 73-6905.

At the center of American fiction is the myth of a young man who,
unable to adapt to society, retreats into the wilderness. Ranging
from Edgar Huntly to Why Are We in Vietnam, the study argues that MD
relocates the myth in a new psychological and metaphysical dimension.
Ishmael is the first wilderness hero to achieve an inner freedom.
(DA: 33-5140)

293. Scorza, Thomas J. Melville's Politics: A Study of Billy Budd,
Sailor. Claremont Graduate School, 1972. 221 pages. Order 72-30,565.

Melville's return to prose in the creation of BB serves as a comment
on the author's career in poetry. Rather than the "testament of
acceptance" or a revolutionary critique, the long tale reveals the
necessity of a tension between philosophy and politics. Melville
demonstrates the superiority of his philosophical poetry by
emphasizing the difference between a philosophically derived reality
and one built upon history, science or religion. (DA: 33-2454)

See: Scorza, Thomas J. "Technology, Philosophy and Political Virtue: The Case of Billy Budd, Sailor," Interpretation, 5, i (1975), 91–107. In the Time Before Steamships: Billy Budd, the Limits of Politics, and Modernity. DeKalb, Ill.: Northern Illinois University Press, 1979.

294. Sweeney, Gerard Michael. Melville's Use of Classical Mythology. University of Wisconsin, 1972. 337 pages. Order 72-9147.

Previously, critics have examined Melville's use of mythology by setting up arbitrary definitions of a mythic figure, such as Prometheus, and then applying those definitions to the works. This study departs from that approach by examining the classical allusions in sources Melville is known or believed to have read. Ahab, for instance, reflects the images of Prometheus in Aeschylus, Robert Burton, and Francis Bacon and of Oedipus in Sophocles. The Orestes myth is strong in P. Overall, Melville's use of the classics diminished in the later works.
(DA: 32-5752)

See: Sweeney, Gerard M. "Melville's Hawthornian Bell-Tower: A Fairy Tale Source." American Literature, 45 (May 1973), 279-85. "Melville's Smoky Humor: Fire-Lightning in Typee," Arizona Quarterly, 34: 371-76. Melville's Use of Classical Mythology. Amsterdam: Rodopi, 1975. Rpt. Atlantic Highlands, NJ: Humanities Press, 1976.

295. Wells, Daniel Arthur. Evert Duyckinck's Literary World, 1847-1853: Its Views and Reviews of American Literature. Duke University, 1972. 391 pages. Order 73-19,517.

Melville is mentioned frequently throughout much of this study of Duyckinck's literary opinions from 1847 to 1853. The editor's early recognition of Melville is discussed, as is the break in 1852 between the two after Melville "had surpassed his mentor intellectually and aesthetically." "Bartleby" is interpreted in light of the break. (DA: 34-1300)

See: Wells, Daniel A. "'Bartleby the Scrivener,' Poe, and the Duyckinck Circle," Emerson Society Quarterly, 21 (IQ 1975), 35-9.

296. Westbrook, Wayne William. Wall Street in the American Novel. Bowling Green State University, 1972. 238 pages. Order 73-1124.

In MD, Melville associates deviltry and finance. "Bartleby" presents a parable of the artist rebuked by commercial society. As evidenced in CM, Melville is the first writer to employ the confidence man archetype, a recurring figure in American financial fiction. HM: 8-13. (DA: 33-3607)

See: Westbrook, Wayne William. Wall Street in the American Novel. New York: New York University Press, 1980.

297. Wright, Ray Gaylon. Herman Melville: The Art of Telling the Truth. Texas A & M University, 1972. 156 pages. Order 72-24,345.

To achieve an artistic whole, Melville balances ambiguity of thought
with clarity of structure. A recurring image which functions as a
controlling structure in most of the works is Initiation. (DA:
33-1151)

1973

298. Abrams, Robert Edward. Leviathan's Maw: Melville's Vision of
Nothingness. Indiana University, 1973. 183 pages. Order 73-12,317.

Melville's works are a search for the aesthetic and psychological
means of coping with his "vision of nothingnesss." The early
voyager-narrators encounter "nothingness" as they lose belief in
traditional systems and prefer to be duped by surface illusions. Yet,
in MD, Melville reaches out for the excitement derived from
"subverting familiar, coherent, everyday reality...." Violation of
traditional systems gives a sense of crossing into new areas of
knowledge. After MD, clearly nihilistic works emerged. The poems and
BB, however, find a view of salvation in this nihilism--an escape into
"an all-transcending nonchalance." (DA: 33-6337)

See: Abrams, Robert E. "'Bartleby' and the Fragile Pageantry of the
Ego," English Literary History, 45: 488-500. "Typee and Omoo: Herman
Melville and the Ungraspable Phantom of Identity," Arizona Quarterly,
31 (Spring 1975), 33-50.

299. Baar, Stephen Ronald. Novel to Film: The Adaptation of American
Renaissance Symbolic Fiction. University of Utah, 1973. 207 pages. Order
73-32,034.

Focusing primarily on The Scarlet Letter, The House of the Seven
Gables, and MD, this study determines whether the film versions
"capture the essential tone, spirit, texture, and themes of the original novels." While less important fiction of the American Renaissance
has been "adapted more readily to film," Hawthorne's and Melville's
works and their sense of darkness resist translation. HM: 143-157.
(DA: 34-4186)

300. Black, Walter Eugene. Failure Redeemed: Melville's Reworkings of
Mardi, Pierre, and Clarel. University of Denver, 1973. 231 pages. Order
73-30,206.

Despite their flaws, M, P, and Clarel reflect major events in
Melville's intellectual and aesthetic life, and Melville intended them
to have important places in his canon. But features meant to provide
this stature create the flaws: epic plots and settings strain the
reader, universalized characters become stereotypes, language designed
to convey the author's earnestness produce disturbing infelicities of
style. Melville redeemed these failures by reworking the same
materials into more polished works. Thus, MD grows out of M,
"Bartleby" out of P, and BB out of Clarel. (DA: 34-3334)

301. Blau, Richard Miles. The Body as Ground of Being in Four Novels of
Herman Melville. Yale University, 1973. 224 pages. Order 74-10,334.

>The body is the boundary between the Me and the Not Me; it separates
>the two yet shares aspects of each. It is a "critical term" through
>which we can understand the failures to unite Me and Not Me as
>recorded in T, WJ, MD, and P. Four sets of paired symbols inform
>Melville's perception of the body: motion and stasis, upright and
>prostrate figures, internal and external space, and the dual functions
>of the senses. Tommo wants to reunify body and mind in a primitive
>world but gets cold feet. White Jacket gains psychic freedom in his
>coat but lets it sink. Ishmael achieves a union of mind and body in
>telling the Ahab tale, but that drama is ironically not his own.
>Fihally, Pierre achieves "a new and wonderful world only to end ... in
>a barren ... isolation." (DA: 34-7220)

See: Blau, Richard. "Melville in the Valley of the Bones," American
Transcendental Quarterly, 10 (Spring 1971), 11-16.

302. Bradley, Donald William. Character as Thematic Embodiment in the
Fiction of Herman Melville. University of California at Riverside, 1973.
260 pages. Order 74-13,556.

>Melville's fiction records the author's growing comprehension of the
>pessimistic view of a deterministic world that victimizes man. His
>heroes manifest this determinism. T and O introduce "rudimentary
>heroes" which display characteristics of the Innocent, the Fugitive,
>and the Victim, upon which Melville rings changes throughout his
>subsequent works. As R improves upon T and O in that it presents an
>admirably sustained "adolescent persona," so does WJ improve upon R by
>deepening the narrator's awareness of death. With Ishmael as Fugi-
>tive, MD introduces Ahab as the Quester. P builds upon this last
>trait and allows Melville to explore new avenues (hereditary and
>environmental influences) of his deterministic theme. "Benito
>Cereno" and IP feature victim-heroes; and M, CM, Clarel, and BB
>present allegorical embodiments of the victim. (DA: 35-440)

303. Chun, Woo Yong. Thought and Structure in Melville's Moby-Dick and
his Later Works. Ohio State University, 1973. 293 pages. Order
74-10,930.

>By examining the shifting relationship between "fictional forms and
>the thoughts that shaped them," we learn that the structural
>disharmonies that characterized many of the works are symptoms of
>uncontrolled tensions between Melville's metaphysical and aesthetical
>concerns. His drive toward realism, or "affection for reality"
>accounts for "the character of his art" after MD which at various
>points erupts into disharmonies that later prove fruitful. Melville's
>initial absorption in metaphysics weakens M which fails to unify its
>quest and satire. MD, however, is more coherent because its form
>grows organically from Ishmael's consciousness. Although structurally
>stronger than M, P reveals Melville's "aesthetic and metaphysical
>paralysis" due to the recognition that fiction itself cannot convey
>truth. The magazine pieces subordinate metaphysics to the mundane as
>Melville's art moves toward realism, empiricism, and objective
>perception. In CM, however, he accepts fiction as "a game of writing"

which he plays "to the hilt." BB subsumes metaphysical concerns in its empirical representation of reality and thus leaves us with a work of art as finely crafted as a "'polished block.'" (DA: 34-7184)

304. Chesler, Pearl Canick. A Correspondent Coloring: Dickens and Melville in Their Time. Columbia University, 1973. 342 pages. Order 76-15,552.

Melville and Dickens are compared in terms of the cultural and historical forces that shaped their lives and their heroes. Unlike the bourgeois British hero who must accommodate his own will to that of society,the American hero grows out of a wilderness experience; he is a self-reliant, self-made man. Melville explores the ideological foundations and cultural assumptions of America's success motif in two autobiographical works. In R, the past fails to guide the future just as the father cannot guide the son. Beyond this, Pierre (in the second autobiographical work) must "create a new philosophy for dealing with his unfathered condition." Also discussed is "Bartleby." (DA: 37-294)

See: Solomon, Pearl Chesler. Dickens and Melville in Their Time. New York: Columbia University Press, 1975.

305. Dussinger, Gloria Roth. The Romantic Concept of the Self, Applied to the Works of Emerson, Whitman, Hawthorne, and Melville. Lehigh University, 1973. 306 pages. Order 74-6680.

Hawthorne's and Melville's dark visions stem not from their Puritan past but from concepts established by the second generation romantics. Here, romanticism is "conscious self-creativity" or a three-part process of creating oneself that runs from experience of the concrete world to abstract thought and back to a more self-conscious form of action. While engaged in this spiral process, the dark romantic must also come to terms with a set of polarities: subject-object, ego-id, and experience-essence. Emerson did so happily in proposing a balance between "public man and private man." Hawthorne and Melville, however, could not go beyond the "empirical," past-bound self, and thus their self-creativity came to "a dead end." Whereas Byron and Poe managed in separate ways to wed self-creativity and rationalism. Hawthorne and Melville, who disliked the concept of self creativity, nevertheless immersed themselves in it. Finally, the study argues that "bright" not "dark" romanticism is the deeper viewpoint, for it addresses and resolves the human condition rather than merely confronts it. HM: 221-85. (DA: 34-5963)

306. Elgin, Donald Deane. The Rogue Reappears: A Study of the Development of the Picaresque in Modern American Fiction. Vanderbilt University, 1973. 328 pages. Order 74-1339.

The picaresque is a continuously evolving tradition in American fiction. Beginning on American soil with Brackenridge's Modern Chivalry, it has become a frequently used vehicle in contemporary fiction. In O, Melville continues this tradition but also demonstrates "the basic incompatability of the picaresque tradition with the traditional American concern for the romantic or quest hero." HM: 48-60. (DA: 34-4256)

307. Engle, Gary. The Face of Ambiguity: A Study of Confidence Men in American Literature before 1900. University of Chicago, 1973. 219 pages.

The confidence man lies somewhere between the picaro or rogue and the criminal, and operates within "the realm of faith." He is amoral, mentally superior, ambiguous, and mendacious. On the surface, he merely reflects of all he meets; beneath the surface he is unknowable. In CM, Melville forces the reader to join the novel's "family of characters," all of whom must confront "the dilemma of belief." Some impose the dilemma on others; some believe but cannot act; some deny the problem exists. The reader's choice is to continue doubting. HM: 90-133.

308. Erdim, Esim. Appearance and Reality in Herman Melville. Ankara University (Turkey), 1973. 214 pages.

As an artist, Melville searches for aesthetic rather than ethical resolutions to the problems of nature and society. WJ, MD, P, and BB reveal the author confronting his readers with situations in which the meaninglessness of all order is presented for the satisfaction or enjoyment derived from having experienced the stories in question.

309. Frederick, Joan. Variations upon a Theme: The Use of Physical Disabilities in Melville's Fiction. University of Tennessee, 1973. 154 pages. Order 74-3820.

Such physically crippled characters as Tommo, Samoa, the top-man in WJ, the cripples in CM, are tied to the themes of the individual novels and to Melville's general theme "of the persistent but unsuccessful struggle of man to understand the nature of the universe in which he has been placed." The cripples represent man as a flawed, imperfect being. A detailed "Table of Contents" provides quick reference to the various characters and disabilities discussed. (DA: 34-5099)

310. Fryer, Judith Joy. The Faces of Eve: A Study of Women in American Life and Literature in the Nineteenth Century. University of Minnesota, 1973. 386 pages. Order 73-25,690.

The woman's place in society was a major topic of concern in the 19th century, but today's critics of that era have focused on the American Adam and ignored Eve. Women appear thoughout 19th century fiction in various roles: temptress, princess, mother, and "new woman." In Pierre, Isabel is the temptress; whereas Lucy is the American princess (Eve before the Fall). HM: 73-85, 130-4. (DA: 34-2558)

311. Gibbs, Charles Kenneth. Myth and Creativity in Moby-Dick. University of Massachusetts, 1973. 211 pages. Order 73-31,090.

Drawing upon the insights of Erich Neumann and Carl Jung, this study examines Melville's use of myths in MD and the nature of his symbolic art. The search for the whale recapitulates in mythic terms Melville's "search for the creative sources of his own imagination." Ishmael represents the passive, unconscious means of tapping creativity; whereas Ahab shows us the aggressive, exclusively conscious way. (DA: 34-4200)

312. Hansen, Klaus Peter. The Process of Communication in the Three Major Tales of Herman Melville. Dusseldorf, 1973. 134 pages. (German).

Wayne Booth's approach is too "static" to explicate the "process of narrative communication" that occurs in "Bartleby," "Benito Cereno," and BB. In each, one subject confronts another "whose extraordinary nature provokes a query into its genesis and being." The thwarted interactions of these narrative elements generate a theme of futility felt in all three tales. (EASG, 1973, item 84)

See: Hansen, Klaus Peter. Vermittlungsfiktion und Vermittlungsvorgang in den drei grossen Erzählungen Herman Melvilles. Frankfurt am Main: Athenäum, 1973.

313. Harris, Duncan S. Melville and the Allegorical Tradition. Brandeis University, 1973. 226 pages. Order 73-15,449.

Melville's use of allegory in the early works was dynamic, and it grew in depth and complexity as Melville developed as a writer. M signals a move from realistic travel adventure into a Spenserian allegorical quest. Melville's reading of Shakespeare and Hawthorne provided the author a more advanced understanding of allegory, and in MD he is able to integrate the allegorical mode in the popular adventure tale, but ultimately an allegorical reading of MD is not possible, for Ahab's allegorical mode of perception is defeated, implying "the rejection of the possibility of allegory" in Melville's world. (DA: 33-6911)

314. Herold, Eve Griffith. A Study of Bildungsroman in American Literature. Ohio State University, 1973. 277 pages. Order 73-26,836.

Two preliminary chapters examine the emergence of the Bildungsroman in the early nineteenth century and its development as an instrument of social criticism related to the increasing primacy of middle-class culture. In R, Melville corrects the optimism of Franklin's Autobiography. In P, the theme becomes "the destructive power of American ideology to so falsify the world as to incapacitate the youth for his encounter with its brutalities." HM: 161-73. (DA: 34-2562)

315. Kaman, John Michael. The Lonely Hero in Hawthorne, Melville, Twain, and James. Stanford University, 1973. 152 pages. Order 74-6494.

Yvor Winters, Christopher Caudwell, and Georg Lukács provide the theoretical grounding for the thesis that the loneliness of the American hero stems from "a pair of relaxed contradictions in his experience": being-consciousness and freedom-necessity. A variety of dialectics in P (aristocracy-democracy, country-town, earth-heaven, Glen-Pierre, Lucy-Isabel) take shape in the novel, patterning themselves on the being-consciousness conflict. Pierre's loneliness is enhanced by the irony that the closer he comes to relatives, the lonelier he becomes. Added to this is a lonely consciousness derived from the transition from feudal to capitalist systems found in the novel. Pierre's sought-for isolation parallels the isolation imposed upon man by capitalism's "atomistic" structure. The novel, then, reveals both the limits of Pierre's vision and Melville's society. HM: 45-79. (DA: 34-5974)

316. Kutrieh, Ahmad Ramez. <u>Melville's The Confidence-Man: The Mode of High Parody</u>. Bowling Green State University, 1973. 164 pages. Order 74-1767.

"High parody is a mode by which beliefs available to the author are represented without being completely adopted or refused.... Melville, uncomfortable in any belief and unable to completely reject, adopts an objective, keen, observing attitude in which he is content to mirror the total picture of his age, feeling that if he cannot answer the questions he encounters, at least he can pose all of them as accurately and as vividly as possible." (<u>DA</u>: 34-5182)

317. Longenecker, Marlene B. <u>The Landscape of Home: Wordsworth and Melville</u>. SUNY-Buffalo, 1973. 253 pages. Order 74-4422.

This phenomenological study of alternative forms of romanticism proposes that the major problem in Wordsworth and Melville is a recognition of "ontological homelessness." Melville deals with the problem through a poetics of discontinuity and a personal revolution (rather than evolution). HM: 122-245. (<u>DA</u>: 34-5110)

318. Lund, Charles Carroll, II. <u>Beholding the Shadows of Fate: "The Town-Ho's Story" in Moby-Dick</u>. Tufts University, 1973. 140 pages. Order 74-2043.

"Shifting patterns of word, image, and theme [make the meaning of "The Town-Ho's Story"] difficult if not impossible to detect." Seeing the story in isolation and as an epitome of <u>MD</u> makes it an illustration of one's own preconception of the novel's meanings. Melville is less interested in the tale's moral concerning the problem of equality of opportunity than in the force behind the quest for the white whale. The study also "[explores] the possible reactions of the reader of <u>MD</u> to his 'wicked book.'" (<u>DA</u>: 34-5110)

319. McMillan, Grant Edgar. <u>"Nature's Dark Side": Herman Melville and the Problem of Evil</u>. Syracuse University, 1973. 271 pages. Order 74-17,598.

Melville's sense of evil develops in two ways; it becomes increasingly more complex and subtle, and it moves from the sociological to the metaphysical. The early works presume to offer sociological solutions to social evils, but by <u>MD</u> Melville had a darker vision of the innate depravity in existence and of man. The later works (including <u>Clarel</u> and <u>BB</u>) confirm this. (<u>DA</u>: 35-1055)

320. Mahony, Catherine Joanne. <u>Ixion's Wheel: Melville's Symbology of Time</u>. Auburn University, 1973. 185 pages. Order 74-11,220.

Time is like a circle in which the circumference is reality and the center is the absolute. Emerson felt that man, residing on the circumference, could connect with the absolute by perceiving "emblems" of the absolute that radiate from the center. Dickinson connected by transcending duration and time altogether. Although Melville's time is also a circle, he is no such transcendentalist. Penetrations toward the center reveal an ever-changing absolute. Melville's questers cannot free themselves from the despair of introversion or "fantastic imagination." Melville's problem of faith then derives from his problem of time. M, MD, P, selected tales, and BB are discussed with respect to each quester's struggle for transcendence in time. (DA: 34-7196)

321. Miller, Arther Hawks, Jr. Herman Melville: A New Biographical Profile. Northwestern University, 1973. 162 pages. Order 73-30,665.

Taken together, Howard's and Arvin's biographies provide (as Stanley Williams points out) "an overall balance" between academic and psychological comments. But they see Melville's life as a building up to and falling away from MD. The stronger critical focus (since the 1920's) on the later works, however, requires a biographical approach that considers the steady purpose of Melville's long career in the pursuit of high literary goals. (DA: 34-3419)

See: Miller, Arthur H. "Herman Melville: A New Biographical Profile," Melville Society Extracts, 15 (1973), 1-11.

322. Moore, Autumn Maxine S. That Lonely Game: Melville, Mardi, and the Almanac. University of Kansas, 1973. 442 pages. Order 73-30,848.

This detailed, allegorical reading of M argues that Melville created a "riddle-game,... a mischievous vengeance against British readers who would not believe that the author of T and O was really an American sailor." Melville used "The American Almanac from December, 1845, through October, 1846, to construct a hidden satire on the themes of revenge and discovery of new worlds." Characters in M have planetary identities and act according to planetary movements of the zodiac. (DA: 34-3350)

See: Moore, Maxine. That Lonely Game: Melville, Mardi, and the Almanac. Columbia, Mo.: University of Missouri Press, 1975.

323. Nechas, James William. Synonomy, Repetition, and Restatement in the Vocabulary of Herman Melville's Moby-Dick. University of Pennsylvania, 1973. 476 pages. Order 74-2434.

Language and theme cannot be separated, and one of the most reliable ways to grasp the theme of a work is through linguistic analysis. Examined here are three habits of diction in MD: repetition, synonomy, and restatement. These are related to Melville's use of negative affix words, his significantly repeated words, and his creation of phrasal epithets. That the whale can be known only in terms of what it is not is expressed through negative affix words. (DA: 34-5196)

See: Nechas, J. W. "The Ambiguity of Word and Whale," College Literature, 2 (1975), 198-225.

324. Palacin, Angeles. La Importancia de Arte Illusionista en Pierre or the Ambiguities, De Herman Melville. Universidad de Madrid, 1973.

The content, reception, and criticism of P are reviewed. Misreadings of the novel derive from two errors concerning the novelist--that he was a romantic and a skeptic. A key element in the novel is its "pictoric illusionism." (Abstract edited from brief extracts of the dissertation translated by the author.)

325. Parker, Bruce Richard. Political Thought of the American Renaissance: Melville and Parkman. University of California at Berkeley (Political Science), 1973.

326. Pryse, Marjorie Lee. The Marked Character in American Fiction:
Essays in Social and Metaphysical Isolation. University of California at
Santa Cruz, 1973. 299 pages. Order 74-16,405.

Eastern philosophies view the isolation of the individual as both a
form of scapegoating which purges society of its guilt and of self-
exploration in which the outcast meditates (à la Maharishi Mahesh
Yogi) upon a "mantra," or touchstone to transcendence. The American
transcendental artist engages in a similar pattern. He is a "marked"
outcast whose search for self-awareness benefits himself and ultimately the society that initially rejects him. Lacking a concrete
analogue to the mantra, however, American artists, nevertheless,
achieve a kind of "transcendental meditation" by gazing at mantras of
their own crafting. While Ahab is marked by his lost leg, Ishmael's
problem lies precisely in the fact that he lacks a "point of reference." (DA: 35-119)

See: Pryse, Marjorie. The Mark and the Knowledge: Social Stigma in
Classic American Fiction. Columbus, Ohio: Ohio State University
Press for Miami University, 1979.

327. Raniszeski, Edward L. The Significance of the Christian Ethic in
Herman Melville's Pierre: Or the Ambiguities. Bowling Green State
University, 1973. 267 pages. Order 73-18,186.

P reveals Melville's "acceptance of the basic tenets of Christian
theology." Its poor reception resulted from cultural and literary
prejudices. In the novel, Melville reviews the alternatives put
before Pierre by his society and, in the end, demonstrates the fallacy
of all except for Christianity. Various characters represent ethical
qualities, and a correlation emerges between "the favor and sympathy
[Melville] shows toward characters and the degree to which they are
Christian." (DA: 34-738)

328. Roche, Arthur John, III. A Literary Gentleman in New York: Evert A.
Duyckinck's Relationship with Nathaniel Hawthorne, Herman Melville, Edgar
Allan Poe, and William Gilmore Simms. Duke University, 1973. 309 pages.
Order 74-1157.

Duyckinck's relationship with various authors helped him realize his
goal of the development of a native American literature. The editor's
early assistance to Melville and his introduction of him to Hawthorne
increased Melville's literary opportunities. HM: 191-239. (DA:
34-4282)

329. Rogers, Jane Ellin. The Transcendental Quest in Emerson and
Melville. University of Pittsburgh, 1973. 189 pages. Order 74-18,413.

Responding to Brodtkorb's phenomenological approach, this study of
Emerson and Melville's quest motif attempts to derive a better recognition of our own "partnership of creation with the artist." In dealing with the "discrepance" between real and ideal, Emerson proposed

the adoption of a "double consciousness" that could contain both but
which for Melville was impossible. A scrutiny of P̲ (its personae,
Plinlimmon, and the Enceladus dream, in particular) indicates that
while Pierre fails to achieve "double consciousness," Melville and the
reader, through the experience of the novel, do. HM: 92-181. (DA:
35-1632)

330. Schwab, Allen Michael. Interrupted Communion with the World. A
Study of Herman Melville's Short Fiction. Tufts University, 1973. 405
pages. Order 74-2050.

The magazine pieces are the medium by which Melville "re-negotiated
the relationship with his material." Three technical problems are
isolated: lack of space to allow for detail and complexity, weak
structural links between the narrators and the protagonists, the
struggle to make form suit content. "Bartleby" and "Benito Cereno"
alone succeed on the terms they establish. B̲B̲ resolves the three
problems. In the "Science Stories" ("The Lightning-Rod Man," "The
Apple-Tree Table," and "The Bell-Tower"), Melville focuses on the
desire for knowledge beyond what is simply measurable. (DA: 34-5203)

331. Selsor, Thomas A. Thematic and Structural Analysis of Billy Budd,
Sailor." University of Wisconsin at Madison, 1973. 271 pages. Order
73-23,085.

There is no easy resolution to Billy's case, and Vere serves to
heighten all aspects of the controversy for the reader. Melville
manipulates the reader's trust despite the narrator's contradictions
and digressions. Critics generally blame or praise Vere's judgment
on the basis of his response to the threat of mutiny, but "in reality
the issues remain unresolvably ambiguous." Vere is also discussed in
terms of Lord Nelson and as a representation of Hobbesean reason.
(DA: 34-5930)

332. Stokes, Charlotte Fowler. Moby-Dick: An Analysis of Minor
Characters. University of Florida, 1973. 226 pages. Order 74-19,191.

The novel's thirty-four minor characters fall into three types: the
New Bedforders and Nantucketers, the Ship's crew, and those met during
gams. The principal modes of characterization are description and
dramatic action. Steering clear of attributing a system of characterization to the cast in "Knights and Squires," the study suggests that
each of these minor characters displays different but "not necessarily
hierarchical" alternative views of reality. Recurring features in all
minor characters are their devotion to Christian belief, their prophetic powers, and their humor. Finally, minor characters serve as foils
for both Ahab and Ishmael. (DA: 35-1062)

333. Stout, Janis Diane Pitts. Sodoms in Eden: The City in American
Fiction Before 1860. Rice University, 1973. 238 pages. Order 73-21,604.

Treatments of the city in American fiction before 1860 are generally
anti-urban. Concerned with alienation, Melville saw the city as a
constriction of possibility. The study examines R̲, P̲, IP̲, "Bartleby,"
and other tales, but only in P̲ does Melville imagine the city as a
place of opportunity, and here only as a thwarted potential. HM:
171-204. (DA: 34-1257)

See: Stout, Janis P. "The Encroaching Sodom: Melville's Urban Fiction," Texas Studies in Literature and Language, 17: 157-74. "Melville's Use of the Book of Job," Nineteenth Century Fiction, 25 (June
1970), 69-83.

334. Straubel, Daniel Charles. The Projection of Melville and his
Concerns as an Author into Mardi. Kent State University, 1973. 174 pages.
Order 73-27,258.

The narrator's search in M parallels Melville's own quest for an
identity as an author. M is a "book about writing a book about characters in action." But, as it progresses, Melville's identification
shifts from Taji to Babbalanja and others. The ending reflects the
resulting ambivalence: the narrator defiantly seeks self-destruction
while Babbalanja turns toward Serenia. M is a rich work, but its
author was "pulled in too many directions to produce a coherent, unified work of art." (DA: 34-2658)

335. Strickland, Carol Ann Colclough. The Search for the Father in Selected American Novels. University of Michigan, 1973. 365 pages. Order
74-15,869.

The paradigm for a youth's successful search for his father involves
three phases: 1) an initial, uninformed identification with
(usually) the biological father, 2) a rejection of that person, and
3) the selection of an "authority figure who embodies the ideals by
which the seeker chooses to live." If this "code" leads to confusion
for the youth, he may follow one of three routes: 1) death or rejection, 2) increased self-reliance but at the cost of social commit-
ment, and 3) a reconciliation. Because Pierre cannot outgrow his
desire for a perfect father, he follows alternatives one and two,
"gaining neither a sustaining vocation, social role, or system of
values." HM: 26-56. (DA: 35-418)

See: Strickland, Carl Colclough. "Coherence and Ambivalence in
Melville's Pierre," American Literature, 48 (1975), 302-11.

336. Waite, Robert George. "Linked Analogies": The Symbolic Mode of
Perception and Expression in Emerson and Melville. University of Kentucky,
1973. 222 pages. Order 74-9325.

Although Emerson and Melville agree that reality is the intersection
of mind and matter, Emerson proposes that the two can be harmonized,
whereas Melville denies that they can. For both, the act of perception is a shaping force. Emerson strives for higher forms of vision
to unite self and world, but Melville fails to believe that "man can
influence his world through an act of will." Melville's notion that
perception creates reality leads him to relativism not idealism, and
the accounts by his early perceiver/narrators become "records of ways
in which to regard the unknown." Also, Emerson's five means of veri-
fying reality as outlined in Nature correspond to traits in Melville's
narrators. Nevertheless, Melville differs again from Emerson in that
his verifications reveal relativism. Finally, the circle imagery
which for Emerson manifests man's expansion toward spirit is for
Melville a metaphor of constriction. Two appendixes annotate readings
dealing with the problem of perception and circle imagery. (DA:
34-6668)

337. Wakefield, John Walter. The Opposing View: A Study of Melville's
Style and Thought. SUNY-Buffalo, 1973. 320 pages. Order 74-4454.

Melville employs "different personas and styles of thought" in order
to break away from the prevailing style of the decorous gentleman and
his optimism initiated by Plato and promulgated by Shaftesbury, Aken-
side, and the Cambridge Platonists. M is not stylistically mature
enough to combine optimistic and pessimistic voices; it remains largely platonic. Ishmael, in his avoidance of logical or systematic
definitions, achieves that stylistic maturity. Connections between
Shaftesbury and Melville's P and CM are explored, and the father-son
relationship among gentlemen forms the context for a concluding commentary on BB. (DA: 34-6669)

338. Welsh, Bernard Howard. Herman Melville as Magian: Zoroastrianism
and Manicheism in the Major Prose Fiction. Auburn University, 1973. 945
pages. Order 73-26,123.

Melville knew more about the specifics of dualist religions than has
been realized. Manicheism is important to Melville as a traditional
heretic outlook in the Middle Ages and in Calvinism. Furthermore, the
incorporation of this dualism in the works (drawn in part from St.
Augustine and Pierre Bayle) is as important as the stylistic
influences of his other reading. In brief, Manicheism provided Melville with a "master metaphor" for balancing good and evil. (DA:
34-2584)

1974

339. Alaimo, Joseph Paul. A Natural History of American Virtue: Melville's Critique of the Transcendental Hero. University of Minnesota,
1974. 374 pages. Order 75-2080.

America's sacred work ethic reflects a number of traditions: medieval
organicism, the Renaissance notion of virtù, and the Calvinist concept
of election. Carlyle's heroic "captain of industry," who in his prophetic mode is a type of David, is an exponent of this ethic. The
first step in his growth is the confrontation of the riddle of the
universe, symbolized in this period by the image of the sphynx. The
protagonists in MD and P serve (respectively) as critiques of
Carlyle's hero and Emerson's version of that hero, the poet; both have
social as well as aesthetic functions. Ahab is a captain of industry
whose failure to cleanse the world and to solve its riddle exposes
"the fatal implications" of Carlyle's and romantic America's dreams.
Pierre's failure is a similar undercutting. HM: 230-362. (DA:
35-5385)

340. Applebaum, Noha. Nature's Cunning Alphabet: Multiplicity and
Perceptual Ambiguity in Hawthorne and Melville. Washington University,
1974. 281 pages. Order 75-14,886.

The technical causes of ambiguity fall into two categories relating
1) to characters (including such devices as supernatural agents and

dreams), and 2) to readers (including the formula of alternative possibilities, linguistic ambiguities, varied reports, unreliable narrators.) Poe's "Ligeia" serves as a model for aesthetic ambiguity, for it requires us to adopt at one time multiple interpretations. Whereas the early works of Melville venture on "epistemological quests," the later fiction attempts to imitate a world of vagueness and ambiguity. CM is the culmination of this "imitative form." Concluding with "Bartleby," the author proposes adoption of the atti- tude that readers of this kind of fiction must be prepared to grasp "irresolvable, alternatively possible explanations." (DA: 36-295)

341. Arac, Jonathan. The Sense of Society in Dickens, Carlyle, and Melville. Harvard University, 1974. 341 pages.

Melville is discussed in relation to English literary culture. He as well as Dickens reflect a third-generation "Carlylean romanticism," wherein the power-driven press gives leverage to common people against the establishment.

See: Arac, Jonathan. Commissioned Spirits: The Shaping of Social Motion in Dickens, Carlyle, Melville, and Hawthorne. New Brunswick, N.J.: Rutgers University Press, 1979.

342. Ausband, Stephen Conrad. A Study of the Mechanistic Imagery in Mel- ville's Fiction: 1849-1857. Tulane University, 1974. 184 pages. Order 74-20,745.

Melville's machine images appear in all his works (except T and O) and imply either the sterility of landscape or the isolation of characters.
(DA: 35-1612)

See: Ausband, S. C. "The Whale and the Machine: An Approach to Moby-Dick," American Literature, 47 (May 1975), 197-211.

342.5 Beidler, Philip Douglas. The Parabolic Design: Self-Conscious Form in American Narrative. University of Virginia, 1974. 366 pages. Order 74-29,210.

Like the shifty confidence of native lore, American writers have dis- tinguished themselves by making their narratives self conscious. Works, like CM, are "open" parables in which the impressions of "authenticity" and "truth" provide both access to and criticism of "larger matters of collective belief." (DA: 35-4498)

343. Bigler, Clair Ellsworth, Jr. A Study of Recurring Imagery of Unusual Height, Depth, and Mass in the Writings of Herman Melville, 1838-1857. University of Wisconsin at Madison, 1974. 350 pages. Order 75-7569.

Melville was profoundly moved by the Egyptian pyramids, and his works can be viewed in terms of a "metaphysics of dimensions" whereby the author created intellectual values out of unusual heights, depths, and masses. The early uses of these unusual dimensions are accompanied by inexplicable feelings of exhilaration. In general, the early fiction- al images represent "pride, joy, liberality, isolation, increased per- ception and danger." In the later images, "perception, isolation, and danger" dominate. (DA: 35-7246)

344. Chitwood, William Oscar, Jr. Symbolism in Melville's Typee and Omoo.
University of Alabama, 1974. 295 pages. Order 75-989.

The idea that Melville's career as a symbolist began with M is undercut by this examination of T and O which, the study concludes, are
more meaningful, more tightly structured, and richer in style than
previously supposed. The juxtaposition of land and sea and of beauty
and death, and the use of the tattoo are symbols that emphasize three
themes: evil, ambiguity, and the hope for an ideal society. T is
treated chapter by chapter; O receives briefer notice. Focusing on
the problem of how symbols emerge from experience, the author isolates
three means of symbol-making that Melville initiates in T and O and
expands upon in later works: they are the use of conventions, "emotional spotlighting" (or investing an object with an emotional aura),
and the use of associations. (DA: 35-7250)

345. Cook, Dayton Grover. The Apocalyptic Novel: Moby-Dick and "Doktor
Faustus. University of Colorado, 1974. 219 pages. Order 74-22,329.

The similarity of the themes and structures in MD and Mann's Doktor
Faustus indicate that both may have been strongly influenced by a
third work, the Biblical Apocalypse. Various chapters delineate seven
characteristics of John's Book of Revelations as they recur in the
featured texts. Apocalyptic structure is tripartite and relies upon
dreams, first-person speakers, and narrative inconsistencies. All
three works create an Arcanum or extreme use of language intended to
express the inexpressible. Although it is not meant to be reducible
to a clear meaning, the Arcanum instills a sense of order and mystery.
The imagery is "monosemous" (allegorical) but also (and largely)
"polysemous" (emblematical). In this context, Ahab's demonism is not
Goethan but Judaeo-Christian (i.e., Apocalyptic). Also discussed are
dualism, teleology, and universality. The study concludes that MD
differs from the Apocalypse in one way; it does not prophesy the
victory of Christ. In this way, MD warns against the hope of the
Millenium. (DA: 35-2260)

346. Fischer, Douglas R. Relativism in Melville's Piazza Tales.
Princeton University, 1974. 254 Pages. Order 75-20,631.

When arranged and read not chronologically but autobiographically, the
early novels reveal a fascination with relativism which in MD becomes
more intense and more clearly pitted against absolutism. PT is
unified in terms of the author's continued reflections on this theme.
Each tale takes on a different problem: "The Piazza" concerns how
people see: "Bartleby," how they feel; "Benito Cereno," how they act
toward each other; "The Lightning-Rod Man," how they believe; and "The
Bell-Tower," how they create. An analysis of "The Encantadas" is not
attempted. The narrator of "The Piazza" is the only true relativist
in the collection of tales, for he can "view both sides of reality as
a constant and constantly evolving whole." (DA: 36-1502)

347. Hayward, Becky Jon. Nature Imagery in the Poetry of Herman Melville.
Duke University, 1974. 182 pages. Order 75-6770.

Melville's poetic technique does not develop much throughout his
career; hence the ideas he wrestles with are best seen in terms of his

treatment of imagery. In pursuit of the recognition that "the reality of life is ... polarity," Melville treats such abstract polarities as good and evil, faith and doubt, life and death with concrete visual imagery, which fall into three categories. The sea's weather, movement, depths, creatures, islands, shipwrecks, and castaways provide fairly conventional images of isolation and chaos. More artful is the use of light and dark which are here classified in terms of various sources of light. Finally, land imagery encompasses animals, plants, edifices, weather, and seasons. (DA: 35-6097).

348. Hurtgen, James Robert. Herman Melville's Political Thought: A Examination of Billy Budd, Sailor (An Inside Narrative). SUNY-Buffalo, 1974. 221 pages. Order 74-19,991.

Rhetoric must be wedded to political science (not just politics). The crafting of a state requires rhetoric that will convey different meanings to different factions. BB's rhetoric "deliberately ... obscure[s] the view of political life embedded in it." In his review of Hawthorne's Mosses, Melville reveals his rhetoric of concealment ("a disinclination to lay bare" the darker side of his thought) which is later employed in BB. Here, the fact that political authority is not divine but merely a human convenience is the bitter truth that must be concealed by a narrator who comments on minor events and yet maintains a godly silence on major events. (DA: 35-1657)

See: Hurtgen, James R. "Melville: Billy Budd and the Context of Political Rule," in Artist and Political Vision, ed. B.R. Barber and M.J.G. McGrath, (New Brunswick, Canada: Transaction Books, 1981), 245-66.

349. Kline, Gary Dean. The Patterns of History in Herman Melville's Clarel. University of Wisconsin at Madison, 1974. 233 pages. Order 75-8625.

The views on Victorian ideology, history, and utopia propounded by R.H. Tawney, Karl Mannheim, and J. Hillis Miller are the backdrop for this discussion of Clarel's characters and "historicism." Two "debates" (between religion and revolution, and over the western movement of civilization) in the poem are intellectual touchstones for all characters. Central to both controversies is the problem of social renewal in the wake of modern cultural dissolution and 19th century subjectivism. Melville opposes the historicist notion that human nature is bound by time and space. Recognizing that history is cyclical in a neutral (not negative) sense, he ackknowleges that permanent social renewal is impossible. Rolfe is the poem's central figure, for although he cannot adopt any ideology, his courage is displayed in his ability to confront all. (DA: 35-7869)

350. Krüger, Harmut. Melville's Ahab and the Problem of Evil--Seen in the Context of the Complete Works and in the Light of Existing Research Studies. University of Kiel, 1974. 347 pages. (German).

An analysis of the evil traits in Jackson, Bland, Radney, Bannadonna, and Claggart shed light upon Ahab and Melville's overall conception of evil. Repudiating "all optimistic and transcendental philosophies of the time," Melville locates evil in man not Nature. Imputing evil in

Nature leads to self-destruction. Finally, Melville's "underlying
conception of life" not any formal problems in his work creates his
well known ambiguities. (EASG, 1974, item 81)

See: Krüger, Harmut. "Herman Melville, 'The Bell-Tower'" in Inter-
pretationen zu Irving, Melville, und Poe, ed. Hans Finger (Frankfurt/
Main: Moritz Diesterweg, 1971), 37-58. Melvilles Ahab und das
Problem des Bösen gesehen im Kontext des Gesamtwekes und im Lichte der
Forschung. Kiel: University of Kiel, 1974.

351. Kwiatek, Vivien Louise. Moment of Truth: The Hunt in American
Fiction. University of Maryland, 1974. 329 pages. Order 74-29,089.

As civilization advances, the atavistic impulse becomes corresponding-
ly more pronounced. In the ritual of the hunt, the hunter identifies
with his prey, faces his inner self, and emerges a better person. The
initiation frequently involves a dark-skinned mentor. The ultimate
horror in the hunt is the hunting of a man or the killing of the
hunter. Treated beside Cooper and Robert M. Bird, Melville in MD is
one of the first to focus his hunt on an animal rather than a man and
to use the motif to clarify problems of the inner being. His hunters
represent both "hard" (savage) primitivism and "soft" (harmony). HM:
21-68. (DA: 35-3749)

352. Leone, Carmen John. Melville's Style in Typee and Moby-Dick: A
Linguistic Analysis. Kent State University, 1974. 158 pages. Order
74-28,280.

The opening of Chapter Two in T and the "Mat-Maker" chapter in MD are
comparable passages stemming from a single experience in the author's
life. Scrutinized under the theories of transformational grammar,
they reveal that Melville uses participles and figurative language
more often in MD. The participle is essentially a truncated sentence
(all verbal, no subject), and the deleted subjects in Melville's
participial phrases are generally some referent to a "superior power
or force." With respect to figurative language, Melville uses twice
as many metaphors in MD than in T, focuses and expands one image
rather than presenting a series of images, and refuses "to violate the
grammatical system" when creating figures of speech. (A metaphor dis-
torts grammar; a simile does not.) A broader examination of both
novels bears out these findings except that the overall ratio of
simile to metaphor in MD (0.18) as opposed to T (0.23) indicates that
Melville may have been more willing to violate grammar in his master-
piece than expected. Ultimately, the evidence supports the notion
that T is factual and MD is romance. (DA: 35-3689)

353. Marino, Bert G. Melville and the Perfectionist Dilemma: A Study of
Melville's Early Religious Thought. Fordham University, 1974. 218 pages.
Order 74-25,068.

Perfectionism is that form of early 19th century revivalism that "put
evangelical counsel ahead of ... natural and ecclesiastical law" and
which (according to Perry Miller and others) shaped most of the
nation's Christian and Transcendental thinking. The problem of
whether man and society are perfectable on earth "here and now"

(immediatism) or after a process of evolution (gradualism) informs much of Melville's first five works. $\underline{T}$ raises doubts as to whether nativism or evangelism can lead to perfection. In $\underline{M}$, the doubts grow into a "metaphysical difficulty." As a "confessional flashback," $\underline{R}$ confronts the problem of misanthropy as the principal "sin" in the perfectionist context, and $\underline{WJ}$ (the culmination of the early works) is Melville's last and most problematic attempt to justify the concept of human and social perfectability. (DA: 35-3690)

354. McColgan, Kristin Pruitt. The World's Slow Stain. University of North Carolina at Chapel Hill, 1974. 258 pages. Order 75-15,674.

Initiation involves the tensions between certain polarities: innocence and knowledge, appearance and reality, evil and the avoidance of corruption, pain and redemption. Unlike Hawthorne who stressed the fortunate fall (through a reliance upon Genesis and Paradise Lost), Melville adopts a more philosophical approach that comes closer to Job and which demonstrates the preponderance of "woe" over "wickedness." Pierre, then, is as much a victim as an initiate. (DA: 36-279)

355. McDonald, Carl Brandt. Narrative of Polarities in Varieties of Psychic Experience: Studies in British and American Romanticism. Florida State University, 1974. 230 pages. Order 75-938.

Romantics are chiefly concerned with "wholeness" (union of mind and nature) or more precisely the "original unity of the psyche" lost by men but which can be retrieved through "the ideal growth of consciousness." Going beyond Jung's analysis of universal symbols and themes, this study advances three forms of psychic experience open to the Romantic. They are given in the form of polarities: 1) relationships of ego and "other" (nature, god, men); 2) the role of ego and the unconscious in finding love, and 3) the potential of the Self to extricate itself from the ego. In that BB demonstrates a freedom of the Self, it is a manifestation of the third polarity. HM: 179-207. (DA: 35-4535)

356. Mitchell, Robin Cave. Omoo and the Development of Herman Melville's Narrative Technique. University of Wisconsin at Madison, 1974. 120 pages. Order 74-19,929.

In $\underline{O}$, Melville initiates a narrative technique that culminates in $\underline{MD}$. After a review of the Omoo criticism, this study focuses on Melville's skill in bridging "the levels of his narrative," i.e., story, digression, factual information, and rambling reflection. Part I of the novel carries on the Typee narrative and demonstrates both control and purpose despite its ramblings. Part II, however, has less narrative and more anecdote. Melville's skill in sustaining the thin narrative is in the facility with which he adopts "the art of transition" and modulates the distance of his narrator. (DA: 35-4441)

357. Mobley, Janice Lee Edens. Eating, Drinking, and Smoking in Melville's Fiction. University of Tennessee, 1974. 147 pages. Order 75-3627.

Melville uses eating, drinking, and smoking for various ends, the least of which is humor. This study steers clear of "metaphysical" allusions to the three habits and deals only with their "literal" appearance in the works which generally promote three themes: abstinence, sociability, and cannibalism. The ambiguity of eating lies in the fact that it is both convivial and self-serving; it is a symbol of brotherhood and yet of cannibalism. (DA: 35-5355)

358. Ormond, Jeanne Dowd. The Knave with a Hundred Faces: The Guises of Hermes in Nashe, Fielding, Melville, and Mann. University of California at Irvine, 1974. 187 pages. Order 75-11,024.

When the rogue-hero of the picaresque begins to realize the full "fictive possibilities inherent in his shabby deceptions," he initiates a development toward the archetypal trickster, Hermes, who traverses both "Apollonian and Dionysian extremes." Although the "hermetic novel" and bildungsroman grow out of picaresque, the former alternative differs from the latter in that its hero never resolves a final identity but in fact "embraces the surface of things and evades the imperative to suffer." Born a bastard and an outsider, the Hermetic hero transcends his suffering by an immersion into a world of bare-faced lies. In this context CM appears as a coherent work which initiates the reader into "the fictive mystery of love," i.e., love's power to bind like and unlike. (DA: 35-7320)

359. Pace, Janyce Akard. Elements of Prophecy in the Prose Fiction of Herman Melville. Oklahoma State University (Education), 1974. 123 pages. Order 76-9743.

According to H. Mears in What the Bible is All About, Old Testament prophets not only predict the future but present a message from God to their own age and to our age. Except for the factor of divine revelation, Melville fits this prophetic mold. His critical pieces reveal a search for truth that labels him both a "forthteller" and a "foreteller." Melville's message to his own age is not revolutionary but one insistent upon democratic reform. His message to our age is a warning against the anti-humanitarian trends of technology. (DA: 36-7424)

360. Pasternak, Dieter. The Problem of Loneliness in the Short Fiction of Nathaniel Hawthorne and Herman Melville. University of Kiel, 1974. 339 pages. (German).

This "systematic analysis" of Hawthorne and Melville examines "types of human isolation" found in their tales and generates from them varying "intellectual backgrounds." Whereas Hawthorne's lonely characters choose to divorce themselves from an established sense of community, Melville's isolatoes have "no such sense of belonging" with respect to humanity or religion. (EASG, 1974, item 84)

361. Reed, Pleasant Larus, III. The Integrated Short Story Collection. Indiana University, 1974. 322 pages. Order 75-8996.

In studying the reasons that a writer may have for arranging their collections of tales, the author briefly discusses the changes Melville agreed to in organizing PT. Land and sea settings are alternated and the elements from the penultimate set of sketches, "The

Encantadas," sum up previously treated isolatoes and prefigure Bannadonna's edifice in "The Bell Tower." Finally, PT's thematic organiza-
tion comes close to that of 20th century collections. HM: 27-32.
(DA: 35-6730)

362. Reynolds, Larry John. A Study of Herman Melville's Views of Man.
Duke University, 1974. 307 pages. Order 75-10,720.

Melville's vacillation between his belief in "unconditional
democracy" and "dislike to all mankind--in the mass" is treated in
this study of his three views of man: man in the ideal, in mass, and
the aristocrat, or uncommon man. The positive democratic view culminates in MD, but the view of mass man, which is derived from Melville's
dealings in life and the literary marketplace, dominates the later
fiction up to 1856. Aristocratic sentiments were nurtured early in
Melville's life and appear throughout the writings. (DA: 35-7267)

See: Reynolds, Larry J. "Antidemocratic Emphasis in White Jacket,"
American Literature, 48: 13-28.

363. Rice, Nancy Hall. Beauty and the Beast and the Little Boy: Clues
about the Origins of Sexism and Racism from Folklore and Literature:
Chaucer's "The Prioress's Tale," "Sir Gawain and the Green Knight," The
Alliterative "Morte Arthure," Webster's The Duchess of Malfi, Shakespeare's
Othello, Hawthorne's "Rappaccini's Daughter," Melville's "Benito Cereno."
University of Massachusetts, 1974. 386 pages. Order 75-16,592.

Folklore, the Bible, and selected literature reveal a fundamental flaw
in Judaeo-Christian society, male domination. The flaw stems from
the fearful association of death and sin with the female (who also is
associated with birth). When the culture makes a beauty (as opposed
to a beast) out of the female, the fear is transferred onto various
"others," principally blacks and Jews. Hence, sexism gives us
racism. In "Benito Cereno," Melville hints that God, a product of a
white male domination, should be denied. (DA: 36-875)

364. Rozenberg, Hélène. A Phenomenological Study of Melville's Clarel.
University of Paris, 1974. 275 pages.

Literature is a form of consciousness; interpretation, according to
Brodtkorb and J. Hillis Miller, is a reliving of the life of the work.
Such an approach applied to Clarel will "lead us to discover an
'original' Melvillean metaphysics." An analysis of two cantos ("The
Hostel" and "Abdon") reveals the poem's chief "problematic": "The
discrepancy between the romance of Christianity and the profanity of
its landscape plunges the soul into a trance of disbelief [which
reenacts] the Passion as it takes the hero, or anti-hero, from life
to Death's door."

365. Scheer, Steven Csaba. Fiction as the Theme of Fiction: Aspects of
Self-Reference in Hawthorne, Melville, and Twain. Johns Hopkins University, 1974. 275 pages. Order 77-16,565.

The novel is "a self referential entity"; its theme is the fiction
making process itself. But because language is a "deceit" or "mask"
the novelist may be imprisoned in his own words. When an artist

becomes self conscious of this process, he rises above the pitfalls of falsely interpreting reality. Reality is the fiction making process itself. In P, Melville uses objects as touchstones of the characters' "hopelessly metaphor-bound inference-drawing mechanisms." In short, they do not mirror reality but the interpretive process of fiction-making. (DA: 38-791)

366. Small, Julianne. Classical Allusions in the Fiction of Herman Melville. University of Tennessee, 1974. 242 pages. Order 74-27,238.

Melville alludes to 318 distinct classical references on 811 occasions throughout the fiction in order to heighten character, imagery, setting, and theme. Classical character types are young men, rebels and sufferers, warriors, thinkers, readers, and women. Classical imagery appears either in clusters to accentuate cultural comparision or randomly to individualize. Melville derives his knowledge of the classics through intermediary sources (Shakespeare) and not from the originals. He had in this respect no more than an average reader's acquaintance with the material. A useful appendix lists all allusions, and charts the ratio of allusions to booklength for Melville's major works. (DA: 35-3701)

367. Smith, Jane Schur. Identity as Change; The Protean Character in 19th and 20th century Fiction. Yale University, 1974. 246 pages. Order 74-24,573.

Homer's Proteus, the form-changing son of a sea god, is a "paradigm of instability and elusiveness" for poets and allegorists, and for modern artists (since the Renaissance) he is both a demonic figure and an admirable example of "fertile multiplicity" well-suited to a world of flux. The archetype provides writers with a range of polarities; the protean character may be free or vulnerable, wise or devious, godly or diabolic. CM is discussed in the context of two other works employing the confidence man figure, and Melville's protean shape-shifter is diabolical. HM: 55-89. (DA: 35-2955)

368. Steele, Betty Jean. Quaker Characters in Selected American Novels, 1823-1899. Duke University, 1974. 157 pages. Order 75-2427.

An examination of the development of Quakerism introduces chapters on fictional Quaker characters as heroes, heroines, villains, and humanitarians. Ahab, Bildad, and Peleg are briefly treated as examples of Quakers who stray from the tenets of their religion. HM: 92-97. (DA: 35-5365)

369. Tumlin, John Sigman, Jr. The Goblet and the Crown: Framing Imagery in the Prose Fiction of Herman Melville. Emory University, 1974. 125 pages. Order 74-18,394.

The experience of navigating the open seas provides Melville with an image that evolves throughout the fiction. The full image involves the flat circle of the ocean intersecting the hemisphere of the heavens with an individual perceiver at the center of the ring. The image appears in fragments (rings, crowns, perceivers) or in the abstract (the apple-tree table, for instance, is a version of the image). (DA: 35-1065)

370. Vella, Michael W. Inner Vision and Society in the American Novel.
University of California at Davis, 1974. 261 pages. Order 75-8363.

A central event in American Protestantism and the American experience
is the antinomian "heresy" which provides a type and structure for a
series of American novels. Various works are treated, then, in terms
of revelation over law, enthusiasm and anarchy, as well as the individual author's religious culture. P (along with works by Howells and
James) not only incorporates the subject of native enthusiasm but also
represents a pivotal point in Melville's career. Exposing the perils
of excessive religiosity, Melville himself suffers, in the poor
reception of the novel, the consequences of his own enthusiasm. HM:
92-142. (DA: 35-6685)

371. Zlatic, Thomas David. Melville's "Pithy Guarded Cynicism": A Study
of his Later Novels. St. Louis University, 1974. 269 pages. Order
75-26,349.

Much of the later work is molded to the thinking of "a laconic,
witty, cryptic, and private sage," one who could "reconcile the
virtues of the serpent and the dove," but also one who must reveal
truth through conscious indirection. From Typee's Kory-Kory to the
Dansker in BB, Melville builds this voice. Also treated are
Babbalanja, Franklin, Jones, Ethan Allen (who is a mythic Christ
figure), and the sloe-eyed boy in CM. (DA: 36-3722)

1975

372. Badal, James Jessen, Jr. Studies in the Tragic Attitude. Case
Western Reserve University, 1975. 276 pages. Order 76-16,031.

Tragedy proper is not merely an artistic creation that adheres strictly to set forms; it is more a matter of an attitude which derives from
a tragic, philosophical view of the universe. The three ingredients
for such tragedy are a hero, an audience, and a conception of universal order. To define tragedy for an age, we must determine that age's
tragic attitude or sense of order. Whereas Sophocles and Shakespeare
shared a distinct attitude with their audiences, Melville could not
and was forced in MD to create his own moral order through Ishmael and
Queequeg. Although madness might reduce the tragic effect of a hero,
Ahab's demoniac spirit deepens the effect in this novel that directly
assaults metaphysical principles. (DA: 37-961)

373. Becker, Carol. Edgar Allan Poe: The Madness of the Method.
University of California at San Diego, 1975. 231 pages. Order 76-2293.

Poe uses insane first-person narrators to parody rational and
analytic thought. The psychological and philosophical ramifications
of this process are examined. Melville shares Poe's distaste for
Cartesian logic; his descriptions of the white whale and the cetological chapters resemble Poe's own anti-rational techniques. HM:
14-77. (DA: 36-5290)

373.5 Bischoff, Joan. With Manic Laughter: The Secular Apocalypse in American Novels of the 1960's. Lehigh University, 1975. 348 pages. Order 75-23,979.

>   CM is the "pivotal text in the history of American apocalyptic fiction. HM: 270-73. (DA: 36-2818)

374. Brent, Julia D. Thomas Carlyle and the American Renaissance: The Use of Sources and the Nature of Influence. George Washington University, 1975. 269 pages. Order 75-18,060.

>   Although Melville came to reject Carlyle's optimisism and metaphysics in general, he shows a familiarity with Carlyle's philosophical, social, and artistic ideas in MD, P, and the tales, but it is as a stylist that Carlyle is most influential. Melville's use of "Carlylese" (characterized by a substratum of 17th and 18th century prose syntax, unusual word coinages, and rhetorical devices employed "according to immediate demands of expression rather than to a larger artistic theme") germinates in M, R, and WJ; reaches full form in MD, and deteriorates in P. The study concludes with a discussion of the nature of influence. HM: 107-207. (DA: 36-884)

375. Bryant, John Lark. Laughter in Darkness: Melville's Use of the Comic in His Later Fiction. University of Chicago, 1975. 280 pages.

>   Whereas Rosenberry concentrates largely upon the growth of Melville's comic spirit and his ability to achieve a balance of comic and tragic visions in MD, this study examines Melville's experiments with the later fiction (1851-1856) in combining comic and serious tones to achieve a mixed tragicomic mode. The works are discussed in terms of structure (genre and narrative devices), characters (genialist, comic isolato, and confidence man), and language. Melville's progress toward tragicomedy begins with P, a novel with clear comic potential that is thwarted throughout by an almost schizophrenic and decidedly humorless, third-person narrator. In the tales, Melville returns to the first-person and recovers his comic sensibility but genial speakers frequently confront "comic isolatoes" or confidence men whose actions and meaning remain inscrutable. The magazine pieces (IP included) constitute a "comic debate" between integrative and subversive comic visions. The two merge with the cosmopolitan in CM, but offsetting this balance is a thoroughly unreliable narrator.

>   See: Bryant, John. "Melville's Comic Debate: Geniality and the Aesthetics of Repose," American Literature, (May 1983).

376. Cabas, Victor Nicholas, Jr. The Broken Staff: A Generic Study of the Problem of Authority in Beowulf, The Tempest, and Moby-Dick. SUNY-Buffalo, 1975. 290 pages. Order 76-9037.

>   Drawing upon an article by Edward Said, the study focuses on "the authority figure" or the author's surrogate to explicate the power of such genres as epic, drama, and novel. In all three, the same two ironic relationships obtain: that which exists between author and authority figure, and that between authority figure and text. In MD, Ishmael is not simply Melville's "doppelganger" but an autonomous

figure who at times expresses the author's view but at time recreates history. Thus, what Ishmael fashions for us at moments of "pessimistic self-reflexivesness" are for Melville "most melancholy," universal truths. This distancing creates a subtle irony further augmented by Ishmael's subordination to Ahab. HM: 200-81. (<u>DA</u>: 36-6654)

377. Caruso, Domenick. <u>A Contemporary Re-Creation of Moby-Dick: An Approach to Creative Writing</u>. New York University, 1975. 479 pages. Order 76-12,572.

A good technique for teaching college-level creative writing courses is to re-create or contemporize an established classic. After analyzing selected critical works on characterization and on <u>MD</u>, the author rewrites <u>MD</u> in today's idiom. The controlling theme of Melville's work is the danger of escaping realities through "bogus mysticism," a theme which speaks clearly to today's fad-oriented society. In the modern remake, Ahab, whose role is reduced and whose whale becomes internalized in his mind, is the mystic. Starbuck is the conventional realist; Stubb, the faddist. Ishmael transcends the problem altogether, and Queequeg is a woman. The opening line--"I didn't know what to make of myself." (<u>DA</u>: 36-8031)

378. Cowan, John Bainard. <u>Moby-Dick as Allegory of the Allegorical Process</u>. Yale University, 1975. 181 pages. Order 76-11,507.

Melville's conception of allegory does not stem so much from the romantics who impute a multiplicity of meaning to an image and who imply that plot is the record of a journey from emptiness to full being; rather it is derived from Christian traditions that begins with Paul (typology) and culminate in Dante. Reading itself is an allegorical process of interpretation. In <u>MD</u>, Ahab is the fated misreader; Ishmael, the deep reader. The novel involves five stages in the interpretive process or "drama of the mind": 1) crossing into a world of purpose, 2) schematizing space and time, 3) self-irony, 4) faith in nature's spirit, and 5) action or history. Also discussed in Melville's treatment of important allegorical patterns: the veil, letter and spirit, and the unlocking angel. (<u>DA</u>: 36-7419)

379. Cuddy, Lois Arlene. <u>Elegy and the American Tradition: Subjective Lyrics on Life and Experience</u>. Brown University, 1975. 322 pages. Order 76 15,621.

An extensive reading of <u>Lycidas</u> yields observations on the elegy as a form that serves as the dominant poetic mode in America. Essentially, elegy exhibits a tension between secular (what is) and Christian (what should be) approaches to earthly problems, in particular skepticism and belief. <u>BP</u> is more about dying than death; for death is a process of living (which includes dying) rather than an autonomous state of being. HM: 171-203. (<u>DA</u>: 37-273)

380. Dea, Eugene Michael. <u>Herman Melville's Clarel: The Final Literary Statement of the Author's Philosophical and Theological Positions</u>. Harvard University, 1975.

As the necessary sequel to <u>MD</u> and the termination of a life-long quest, <u>Clarel</u> anticipates the conclusions of 20th century existent-

ialism. Questions formed in MD are answered in the long poem and
later applied in BB. Melville's conclusions are that there is no God,
religions are spurious, misery is man's natural condition, good and
evil are common natural phenomena, life is bearable when one respects
the life and rights of others, love is no panacea, and death is life's
controlling force and finality. An appendix considers the issue of
homosexuality in Melville's life and work. Here, too, the Melville-
Clarel and Hawthorne-Vine relationships are discussed.

See: Dea, Eugene M. "Evolution and Atheism in Clarel," Melville
Society Extracts, 26: 3-4.

381. Fagan, David Lloyd. The Voyager to Easter: Melville's Resolution of
Doubt and Belief. Florida State University, 1975. 191 pages. Order
75-26,768.

Doubts about the ability to attain the Ultimate Truth plagued Melville
throughout his career. CM marks the lowest point; Clarel, a slow
return to God; and BB, a full rediscovery of religion. (DA: 36-3712)

382. Fannin, Alice. Through a Glass Darkly: Masks, Veils, and Masquer-
ades as Obstacles to Perception in the Major Novels of Herman Melville.
University of Kentucky, 1975. 230 pages. Order 77-5687.

As Melville's doubts about his ability to perceive truth and to reveal
knowledge increase throughout his fiction, his use of mask imagery
becomes more pronounced. Masks appear sparsely in T, and the authorial voice substantiates the existence of a meaning behind these masks.
M's masks are more problematic, but truths can be found behind them.
Ishmael, however, learns not to presume any final truths, and Pierre
further perceives that there are limitations even on the authorship of
masks. CM's masks project an utterly inscrutable world. (DA:
37-5826)

383. Finholt, Richard David. The Murder of Moby-Dick: Mad Metaphysics
and Salvation Psychology in American Fiction. Northern Illinois
University, 1975. 218 pages. Order 76-9864.

The origins of blackness in those American authors who dive are not in
mordid Byronics but in the fact that these "deep thinking minds are
naturally drawn" to the mysteries of the inner self. Ahab is not mad;
he is a messiah who eradicates for us the fear of death. In the
context of Frye's description of the comic nature of melodrama, MD may
be taken as being in the "the ironic, comic, chattering-monkey mode."
HM: 78-107. (DA: 36-7428)

383.5 Freeman, Marsha Aileen. Newton Arvin: A Career in American Letters.
University of Pennsylvania, 1975. 255 pages. Order 75-24,068.

Arvin's biography of Melville was the "best-received" of the critic's
works. HM: 183-90, passim. (DA: 36-2819)

384. Fulcher, James William. The Mask Idea in Selected Fiction of Poe,
Melville, and Twain. George Peabody College for Teachers, 1975. 120
pages. Order 76-3723.

A study of 19th century philosophers reveals two relationships
concerning masks and truth: to find truth you must either break the
mask or wear it. Five themes occur in both orientations: 1) initial
bewilderment over the existence of masks, 2) recognition of the
appearance/reality disparity, 3) unity as a hidden reality, 4) ontological struggle, and 5) the options of optimism and pessimism. Melville resolves apparent inconsistencies in believing and not believing in a reality behind the mask in his "dialectical pattern of consciousness of the mask idea." He fuses the separate concepts of penetration through and concealment of masks in the notion of accepting a
purposiveness in the mask with "a wary confidence." HM: 43-72. (DA:
36-6082)

385. Harris, Peter B. Melville: The Language of the Visible Truth.
Indiana University, 1975. 261 pages. Order 75-17,015.

Melville began his career attempting to tell the "unvarnished truth,"
but as early as M and by the time he wrote "Mosses" he was convinced
that fiction was the only means of conveying the truth. The later
works present a variety of approaches to the creation of "original
art." (DA: 36-888)

386. Hauser, Helen Ann. A Multi-Genre Analysis of Melville's Pierre: The
Patterns Almost Followed. University of Florida, 1975. 220 pages. Order
76-4240.

The storied ambiguities of P are attributable, in part, to the
tensions that arise among a variety of genres that the novel adopts
and maintains concurrently. P bears some resemblance to the novel of
manners and modifies aspects of the gothic novel. As a satire, it
attacks existing norms but fails to offer new ones, and it borrows
much from Elizabethan tragedy. P also presages two modern genres, the
psychological and symbolist novels. (DA: 36-5296)

See: Hauser, Helen A. "Spinozan Philosophy in Pierre," American Literature, 49: 49-56.

387. Hewitt, Elizabeth Chapman. Irony, Protest, and Prophecy in Melville's First Six Books. Tufts University, 1975. 187 pages. Order
75-19,266.

Melville is a "humane artist lacerated by injustice, suffering, and
cruelty," and he uses heavy doses of irony to protest social ills. To
a smaller but no less important degree, he stands as a prophet. T and
O are open works of portest. M reveals America to be the only hope
for man. R and WJ carry on this optimism. In all five, protest is a
straightforward dialectic with the narrative, but in MD protest is
buried covertly within the text and prophecy is made symbolic. (DA:
36-1505)

388. Hinman, Mary-Lou. The Yankee Peddler: His Role in American Folklore
and Fiction. University of Connecticut, 1975. 195 pages. Order 76-1678.

The Yankee peddler is a satiric not comic figure, a moralizer who
teaches by tricking. Melville's use of the figure in CM signals the

figure's shift from hero to anti-hero and heralds a new age of trick-
sters who have few if any redeemable features. HM: 148-185. (DA:
36-5297)

389. Hooson, Christopher John. The City in the 19th Century American
Novel. Indiana University, 1975. 254 pages. Order 75-23,477.

In general, American writers' use of the city moves from early, dream-
like fantasies to realism. For Melville, the city of Liverpool in R
is an occasion for exposing the positive and negative features of
American civilization. HM: 89-123. (DA: 36-2821)

390. Joswick, Thomas Philip. The Unreturning Wanderer: Melville's
Thematics of Origin. SUNY-Buffalo, 1975. 195 pages. Order 76-1450.

For Melville, "the real crisis of man's identity" is the problem of
origin. Two origin myths are explored: that of an autochthonous
genesis (here meaning an origin in nature without forebears) and that
of a genealogical origin. In either case, the problem is that when an
origin is sought, it disappears; but art (the telling of the quest)
begins. Form, then, derives from consciousness, that something which
exists between an origin and an end. Melville's consciousness is not
clear on either origin myth, and his fictive creations have little
sense of an ending. His narratives tend to "pick to pieces" what is
reality, and then to refuse those pieces. (DA: 36-4492)

See: Joswick, Thomas P. "Typee: The Quest for Origin," Criticism,
17 (1975), 335-54. "The Incurable Disorder in 'Bartleby the Scrivener.'" Delta, 6: 79-93. "Figuring the Beginning: Melville's The
Confidence-Man," Genre, 11: 389-409.

391. Kehler, Joel R. A House Divided: Domestic Architecture as American
Romantic Subject and Symbol. Lehigh University, 1975. 325 pages. Order
75-23,995.

A "double consciousness" exists in the American conception of domestic
architecture which stems from the impulses to "make a home within the
House of Nature" and to create the tradition-bound House of Man. Melville created in his tales an extensive pattern of symbols relating to
both design concepts. If one were to reconstruct a "house" from Melville's details, the result would involve four components: a cellar
(the past, unconsciousness), a ground floor (hearth, domesticity), a
garrett (consciousness, ambiguity), and a Tower (dreams, imagination.)
HM: 259-292. (DA: 36-2823)

See: Kehler, Joel R. "Faulkner, Melville, and a Tale of Two Carpent-
ers," Notes on Modern American Literature, 1: item 22.

392. Kemper, Kristie Anne. The Search for a Political Theory in the
Fiction of Herman Melville. University of Tennessee, 1975. 234 pages.
Order 76-1956.

An opening chapter on Melville and politics shows the author was particularly aware of 19th century political developments. Following
chapters treat monarchy in the early works, totalitarianism in MD, and

democracy throughout the canon. Although Melville does not promote
one form of government over another, he continually adheres to the
ideals of the American dream. (DA: 36-4492)

393. Klopf, Dorothy C. The Ironic Romance Tradition in America. Cornell
University, 1975. 368 pages. Order 76-8139.

A romance is ironic when it is skeptical of a culture's new myths.
The basic tension exposed here (rooted in the Puritan experience) is
that between nominalism and antinomianism. Whereas P is a critique of
the former, it is not an endorsement of the idealism of the latter.
(DA: 36-6684)

394. McDonald, Dorothy Ritsuko. The Captive King: The Persistence of
Symbolic Memory in Herman Melville. University of California at Berkeley,
1975. 419 pages. Order 76-723.

A stable culture surrounds and protects the self like a secure wall or
enclosure. "Cultural failure ... is the failure of a culture to
protect the self against the destructive forces ... found in nature
and in man." Melville's works abound in decaying walls and enclosed
gardens which, respectively, hint at the decay of culture but also the
remembrance of a true culture. Also, the image of the golden lizard
represents the purity of the self. (DA: 36-4493)

395. McGuire, Peter Joseph. Herman Melville's Clarel: The Repudiation of
Myth. Brown University, 1975.

396. McIntire, Mary. The Buried Life: A Study of The Blithedale Romance,
The Confidence-Man, and The Sacred Fount. Rice University, 1975. 243
pages. Order 75-22,039.

The novels treated "explore ... the tension between the individual,
unreliable consciousness and the social masquerade," which results in
the formal creation of an alienated narrator who promotes an alternate
(but not always verifiable) vision that extends beyond the vision of a
"shifting, ambiguous world." Seen as both a metaphor of reality and
as a parody of the Victorian novel, the social masquerade in CM is a
play and a riddle that challenges and thereby asserts a corrective
influence upon the reader. HM: 101-190. (DA: 36-2183)

397. McKinney, Jill Louise. Herman Melville and the Law. University of
Pennsylvania, 1975. 355 pages. Order 76-3193.

Melville was deeply influenced in his thought and work by the legal
system of his day. Early on, he learned the value of a lawyer's
approach to problem-solving; indeed, many of his family and friends
were in some way engaged in the law. Melville's literary use of ambivalence reflects the influence upon him of the rules concerning the
judging of the reliability of evidence, the problems of law and epistemology, and law reforms which characterized the "Formative Years" of
American Law (1820-1860). Ahab's monomania may be seen in the light
of two murder cases involving "paranoid monomaniacs," and BB is rein-
terpreted with Lemuel Shaw as a possible source for Vere. (DA:
36-5299).

398. Mitchell, Lee Clark. The Vanishing Wilderness and Its Recorders: Developing Apprehensions about "Progess" in 19th Century American Literature. University of Washington, 1975. 362 pages. Order 75-28,403.

Americans were less enthusiastic and more critical of "progress" and the diminishing wilderness than has been previously assumed. Various painters and literary artists throughout the century translated the impulse toward "cultural relativism" into their art by attempting to "fix" the image of the West as it was fading. Melville's early works can be seen in this cultural context. The author's "descriptive accuracy" in T and O derives, in part, form his recognition that the island life he depicts (like the American wilderness) was passing away. His respect for native life (similar to the complaints of those who mourned the decimation of the American Indian) in MD and CM confirms Melville as a "sophisticated" cultural relativist. HM: 142-173. (DA: 36-3658)

399. Nesaule, Valda. The Christ Figure and the Idea of Sacrifice in Herman Melville's Billy Budd, in Graham Greene's The Potting Shed, in Fedor Dostoevskij's "The Dream of a Ridiculous Man." Indiana University (Comparative Literature), 1975. 129 pages. Order 76-2870.

The Passion of Christ as a plot device, the theme of Christ's self sacrifice as a form of characterization, and the figure of Christ as a symbol of the self are the three approaches employed in the discussion of three works. The typology of sacrifice figures most prominently in BB. HM: 24-43. (DA: 36-5284)

400. Philipp, Friedemann. The Figure of the Skeptic in the Works of Herman Melville: Problems of Literary Form and Ideological Background. University of Kiel, 1975. 221 pages. (German).

An investigation of structural motifs "reveals that Melville's first-person narrator is a skeptic who is invariably contrasted with the Romantic hero. Melville's skeptic is a 19th century creation carrying on an issue first pondered in the Englightenment. The figure is not only a critic of religion, politics, culture, and social structure; he is an "admonisher and prophet." (EASG, 1975, item 86)

401. Pollard, Carole Ann. Melville's Hall of Mirrors: Reflective Imagery in Pierre. Kent State University, 1975. 195 pages. Order 75-27,822.

Melville's reflective imagery (chiefly that of portraits and faces) serves various functions: it deceives and bewilders the perceiver/reader, provides insight by supporting moral decisions, accompanies and causes action, and emphasizes psychological aspects. Generally speaking, a tableau involving a contemplator and the object of his contemplation which often answers problems is a recurring device throughout P. Also, "literary reflection" reveals implications to the reader that are not perceived by the character. Chapters explore reflective imagery as it reveals Pierre's idealism, the themes of incest and narcissism, and the influence of Hawthorne's "Monsieur du Miroir" and Dante's Inferno. (DA: 36-3717)

402. Portales, Marco Antonia. The Old Man in Classic American Literature.
SUNY-Buffalo, 1975. 304 pages. Order 75-18,829.

American's youth consciousness reaches back to the writings of the
Mathers and Franklin, and the representation of old men in our literature often provides insights into this predisposition. Our old men
must be rebelious to be of any interest, and their rebellion is generally against the onslaught of old age. Ahab is one such "young old
man." (DA: 36-1508)

403. Sherrill, Rowland A. "The Span of Portents": The Meaning of
Transcendence in the Fictions of Herman Melville. University of Chicago
(Divinity), 1975.

See: Sherrill, Rowland A. The Prophetic Melville: Experience,
Transcendence, and Tragedy. Athens, Ga.: University of Georgia
Press, 1979.

404. Stewart, Rachel Whitesides. The Conditional Mood of Melville's
Poetry. University of Colorado at Boulder, 1975. 258 pages. Order
76-3957.

The conditional mood is both a grammatical structure and a psychological frame of mind conducive to doubt. Contrary to early criticism
which argued for affirmative readings of the poems, this study
stresses Melville's emphasis upon doubt. A close reading of "Billy
in the Darbies" reveals discords which in turn symbolize the unresolved moral problems of BB. A lengthy discussion of Melville's use of
dramatic monolog shows that the poet attempts to suppress himself and
give voice to various "separate selves." A final chapter discusses
voice and distancing. The poems re-emphasize that Melville's poetic
goal was dramatic/objective not lyrical/subjective. (DA: 36-5305)

405. Wasilewski, William Henry. An Investigation of the Satellite Poems
in Melville's Clarel. SUNY-Binghampton, 1975. 396 pages. Order
75-15,740.

Satellite poems are those poems recited or songs sung by Clarel's
guides and fellow travelers. As "a self-contained unit" within a long
narrative poem, each of the 45 pieces attempts to educate the student
in one of many forms: love song, hymn, bawdy song, dirge, etc. Each
poem is examined within the context of the larger narrative. (DA:
36-290)

See: Wasilewski, William H. "Melville's Poetic Strategy in Clarel:
The Satellite Poems," Essays in Arts and Sciences, 5: 149-59.

406. White, Julie Belle. A Rhetorical Criticism of Moby-Dick: The
Persuasive Campaigns of Ahab, Starbuck, and Ishmael According to their
Substances, Dynamics, and Strategies. University of Minnesota, 1975. 384
pages. Order 76-14,978.

MD lends itself to three rhetorical approaches: eclectic (which
involves psychological, linguistic, and sociological criticism),
evolutionary (communication as process), and valuative (rhetoric as a
value system). All three forms encompass three "senses of rhetoric"--

substantial, dynamic, and strategic. By examining the value systems
that Ahab (the militant), Starbuck (the moderate), and Ishmael (the
antagonistic-transcendentalist) display and how they interact with
each other, other crew members and the reader, the study concludes
that all three voices have equal dominion. The reader is left with a
"cacophony of rhetorics." (DA: 37-35)

407. Zessin, Bruce Delmar. Images of the Artist in 19th century American
Fiction. University of California at Los Angeles, 1975. 210 pages. Order
76-8286.

Three little-known novels by Allston, Willis, and G.W. Curtis yield
themes and characterizations of the artist that are typical throughout
the better known literature. Art, itself, is both a sacred, idealistic calling and a road to wealth. The artist may appear as a victim, a
villain, or a foil to the business man. Lombardo in M is an artist
goaded by necessity, just as Pierre is equally troubled by society.
Bannadonna in "The Bell-Tower" is Melville's only artist-villain.
(DA: 36-6693)

1976

408. Adkins, Stephen Douglas. A Selective Annotated Bibliography on
American Literary Romanticism. Ohio State University, 1976. 377 pages.
Order 77-3473.

Melville ranks beside Emerson and slightly below Hawthorne and Poe as
one of the top four writers mentioned most frequently in the 1200 or
so works on Romanticism cited. (DA: 37-5116)

409. Albert, Theodore Gibbs. 1. The Law vs. Clarissa Harlow. 2. The
Pastoral Argument of The Sound and the Fury. 3. Melville's Savages.
Rutgers University at New Brunswick, 1976. 150 pages. Order 76-26,983.

Rousseau's conception of the primitive as a noble savage and child of
nature conformed nicely to the white America's experience. Because
the savage Indian was defeated, he was made noble. Because the black
man was enslaved, he was made into a willing, submissive child.
Added to this is the stereotype of the Satanic savage. In T, MD, and
"Benito Cereno," Melville debunks these stereotypes to form a "broadly
tolerant human vision." CM is not discussed. HM: 113-42. (DA:
37-3601)

409.5 Auer, Michael Joseph. Angels and Beasts: Gnosticism in American
Literature. University of North Carolina at Chapel Hill, 1976. 232 pages.
Order 77-2018.

Since the true self has no connection to matter, Gnostics are commit-
ted to the destruction of the body, either by a denial or glutting of
the flesh. An alternation between asceticism (angelism) and libertin-
ism (bestialism) is typical of such American gnostics as Poe, Emerson,
Dickinson, and Whitman. Melville runs counter to this concept, for
although he searches for the transcendent, he sees man as rooted in
time and space. (DA: 37-5117)

410. Bohrer, Rand Edward. The Universal Cannibalism of the Seas: The
Development of Melville's Mythology of Alienation. Yale University, 1976.
352 pages. Order 76-29,814.

Traditional conceptions of alienation (Romantic, existential, and
Marxist) cannot account for the peculiarities of Melville's isolatoes
who like Queequeg are paradoxically alienated yet integrated with
nature. The paradox is resolved in much the same way that Melville
resolves the problem of cannibalism. Man is a part of a world in
process which continually reproduces itself by continually consuming
itself. The cannibals in T, Queequeg, the devouring hunt in MD, and
the false, optimistic American society in CM reveal the stages of
development (germinal, mature, and late) of Melville's conception.
(DA: 37-4349)

411. Cok, Georgette Weber. The Allegorical Mode in American Fiction.
CUNY, 1976. 344 pages. Order 76-10,640.

Americans have found expression for their impulses to affirm ideals,
embrace the world of art, and defy history's denial through the mode
of allegory. It is a form that allows the anxious artist to resolve
conflicting world views. At the heart of America's allegorizing is a
predilection for problem solving and a search for self identity that
derives from the Puritans. While Melville's works employ allegorical
doublings (as in "Bartleby") and attempts by rational mediators to
interpret symbols (as does Ishmael), they do not leave us with any
affirmative stance characteristic of allegory. Only in the final
scene of "Bartleby" does Melville successfully achieve a new mood of
acceptance. HM: 83-144. (DA: 36-8056)

412. Coonan, Michael. Spending Light: A Consideration of Refractory,
Binomial Pluralism in Herman Melville's Fictional First Half Days.
University of Pittsburgh, 1976. 642 pages. Order 77-15,154.

Like myths, novels are recreations of the world. This study which
projects three more chapters (two on MD and a conclusion) still to be
written and which lacks a complete list of references cited argues
that Melville's "Art is pluralist" just as all things are. (DA:
38-260)

413. Curry, Steven Scott. The Literature of Loss: A Study of 19th
Century English and American Fiction. University of California at Davis,
1976. 190 pages. Order 76-20,984.

Society by nature thwarts an individual's pursuit of "authentic"
existence, and literature is a defense against the sense of loss
derived from the disintegration of the human community. The experience of loss involves three patterns of imagery: the possession of
space, the figure of the orphan, and the conflict between "letter" and
"spirit." Vanity Fair and MD are treated together as "world-fiction,"
a form that attempts to "describe how and what the world means." They
are self-conscious narratives, without heroes, wherein "the possibility of community" is lost. The author applies Tony Tanner's thesis
that MD is about the process of naming to Vanity Fair. Ahab and Becky
both fail in realizing their separate obsessions because they do not
realize that their "process of calling" is limited. HM: 121-45.
(DA: 37-1529)

414. DiMaggio, Richard S. The Tradition of the American Gothic Novel.
University of Arizona, 1976. 203 pages. Order 76-16,238.

    The elements of the gothic and the development of the British gothic
novel provide a context for this study of the transplantation and
further growth of the form in America. Various components of the
American experience (including the Puritan vision and penchant for
allegory, skepticism, and the Salem witch trial) made the form particularly conducive to Americans, and it has prospered from Brockden
Brown to Robert Penn Warren. Although P takes the Gothic to its deepest levels, the novel fails because of its "bitter skepticism, and
uncompromising darkness." HM: 116-38. (DA: 37-307).

415. Duban, James. Melville and Christianity: His Masquerade. Cornell
University, 1976. 315 pages. Order 77-5738.

    Selected works indicate Melville's steady conservative campaign
against those who would lessen the Calvinist vision of evil. Redburn
is no American Adam. Contrary to the millenialist belief, the new
world has its own share of sin, and Redburn (as he reflects Jackson)
perceives that Augustinian truth. Ishmael reduces to absurdity provi-
dential thought. Pierre castigates two Emersonian premises: intui-
tive epistemology and the soul's perfectibility, and CM undercuts
Arminianism and Unitarianism by showing man to be incapable of distinguishing right from wrong. (DA: 37-5825)

    See: Duban, James. "The Spenserian Maze of Melville's Pierre,"
Emerson Society Quarterly, 23: 217-25.

416. Emery, Allan Moore. Parables of Perception: A Contextual Approach
to Melville's Short Fiction, 1853-56. Cornell University, 1976. 280
pages. Order 77-18,871.

    At the core of each tale in PT is a body of allusions which yields the
philosophical and psychological context upon which the tale was
composed. At war in "Bartleby," for instance, are irreconcilable
elements (the thought of Edwards vs. Priestley's, the Irvingesque vs.
the Poesque) which, like the lawyer and scrivener, disturb each other
yet never resolve themselves. This "confrontation between opposing
perspectives" recurs throughout the tales. (DA: 38-1387)

417. Fineman, Daniel David. On Errands of Life: Vitality and Language in
the Novels of Herman Melville. Princeton University, 1976. 384 pages.
Order 77-4784.

    Melville expected his readers to share with him "the responsibility of
making language live." To "revitalize the language," he continually
tried to break the reader's "habits of mind" while making his texts
salable. His works, then, are both mechanical and yet full of awareness. Melville's process of "defamiliarizing" involves using implaus-
ible facts (cannibals, white whales, etc.) and accidents within the
plot. The revitalizing in T stems from Melville's recognition that he
had to expose "the nudity under the 'covers' of civilization." M
parodies the author's relation to the public; the vitality of WJ and
MD draws from the Greek ideal of art as experience, but Pierre is

incestuous and similarly Melville feeds off himself to make "a book of his life." The subject of CM is the audience's failure to preceive. (DA: 37-5826)

418. Friedman, Andrea Marian. Driven by That Density Home: Herman Melville, Charles Olson, Robert Creeley, and the Problem of Knowledge in a World of Flux. SUNY-Buffalo, 1976. 233 pages. Order 76-20,520.

"Home" is that which is most essentially "human," and "density" is both individual and communal in that one cannot reach home unless everyone reaches home. The crucial experience that recurs in Melville's works is the confrontation of the new and strange with an unprepared and unsuspecting character. Melville, whose "home" is his carpet-bag-ego is able to survive in this world of flux. After a discussion of Charles Olson's and Robert Creeley's responses to these problems and to Melville, the study concludes by addressing the problem of how to teach literature. (DA: 37-2893)

419. Fussell, Mary Burton. Last Testaments: Writers in Extremis. University of California at San Diego, 1976. Order 77-10,637.

Like Fitzgerald and James, Melville left his last work, Billy Budd to us in textual disarray. Supplementing the Hayford-Sealts text with related material discovered on the backsides of old poems, the author considers Melville's "last literary testament" to be more than a self-analysis; it deals with the nature of art. (DA: 37-5814)

See: Fussell, Mary Everett Burton, "Billy Budd: Melville's Happy Ending." Studies in Romanticism, 15: 43-57.

420. Gossom, Deborah Decker. Innocence and Inexperience in Melville's Fiction. Indiana University, 1976. 211 pages. Order 76-21,581.

Innocence is static and ill-suited for the comprehension of reality, which requires more dynamic forms of experience. Although Melville dismisses innocence in T, he returns to the issue wistfully at first but later in a spirit of disillusionment and condemnation. While the innocents in R and WJ adapt, on the one hand, to life's superficialities and, on the other, to deeper issues of self and community, Delano and Billy Budd are imperceptive, unadaptable, incommunicative, and in the latter character, inexplicably violent. (DA: 37-2179)

421. Gray, Valerie Bonita. Invisible Man's Literary Heritage: "Benito Cereno" and Moby-Dick. Ohio State University, 1976. 151 pages. Order 77-10,534.

Ellison hoped in his work to return to the fundamental problems of democracy expressed in the best 19th century fiction, especially that of Melville. While both artists condemn the people, they "affirm the principle" of democracy. The two are also linked in their use of ambiguity, masks, shape-shifting, and the notion of a fluid reality. The problem of racism is one of perception for both, and, themes aside, the two employ similar methods: bird imagery and a mode of perceiving life by concentrating on a unique symbolic world (Ellison's circus and Melville's cetology). (DA: 37-7129)

422. Kelly, Robert Alan. The Prophetic Figure in Herman Melville's Writing. Louisiana State University, 1976. 158 pages. Order 76-25,270.

Melville's use of prophetic characters serves as an index of his skepticism toward the existence or power of God. Although aware of the uncertainties involved in the ideal quest, Babbalanja is a clear, cautionary prophet, perhaps Melville's only forthright example of the type. Ishmael's continual qualifications make him only a part time prophet. Pierre, the absolutist, sees divine will but in the wrong place, and the confidence man's undermining of faith discloses the futility of prophecy. But the return of the narrator in BB to an Ishmaelian vision indicates the prophecy may never be complete; it can only hint at reality's dualistic nature. (DA: 37-2872)

423. Kolvig, Eric William. Young Life's Old Routine: Patterns of Initiation in Herman Melville. Yale University, 1976. 344 pages. Order 76-30,249.

Without set rituals, modern society must rely upon its authors to provide forms of initiation both secular (serving to socialize) and sacred (performing palingenesis, or reenacting creation). Melville obliges the reader by providing us fragments of initiations in the early works. Tommo escapes incorporation into primitive society with his final violent act and thereby initiates himself back into white civilizations. Repeating this theme, O and M show young initiates searching for and failing to find alternatives to their own racial and national destinies. Old patterns of initiation emerge in R, WJ, and MD when heroes attempt to initiate themselves into transcendental realms. After MD, initiations generally fail. (DA: 37-4353)

424. Kountoupes, Gus George. Method and Meaning in Melville's Short Ficiton. University of Toledo, 1976. 180 pages. Order 77-369.

Three neglected tales are examined with respect to Melville's literary aesthetic of truth-telling through indirection (as laid out in "Mosses" and "The Piazza"). The narrators of "Jimmy Rose," "I and My Chimney" and "The Apple-Tree Table" inspect objects or other characters to find "knowledge of immortality," but behind the pleasant surfaces of the observed, the observer ironically stumbles upon a background of darkness that is undefinable. (DA: 37-4354)

425. Magretta, Joan Barbara Gorin. The Iconography of Madness: A Study in Melville and Dostoevsky. University of Michigan (Comparative Literature), 1976. 189 pages. Order 76-19,181.

The biographical approach to Melville's and Dostoevsky's fascination with madness ignores the artful function of madness in exposing the contradictions of the age. After elucidating the history of madness up to the 19th century, the study pairs works by the two authors and discusses the culturally defined models of madness in each pair that allow the artists to explain various "personal responses to the life of unreason." "Bartleby" and "Notes from Underground" present madness in terms of the limits of reason; it preserves humanity. P and The Idiot explore the discontinuous self and show the reader that madness is both a recognition and escape from the human condition. MD is compared to Crime and Punishment and The Brothers Karamazov to show

madness of the autonomous self and the notion that madness is in fact
rooted in the culture. Finally, CM and The Possessed, both nihilistic
works, portray the madness of alienation and unbelief. (DA: 37-1533)

See: Magretta, Joan, "Radical Disunities: Models of Mind and
Madness in Pierre and The Idiot," Studies in the Novel, 10: 234-50.

426. Moore, Richard Sinclair. Melville's Aesthetics of Nature. Duke
University, 1976. 331 pages. Order 76-27,983.

The "picturesque" in American aesthetics unites the wild topography
of the sublime in the background with an agrarian or pastoral fore-
ground and in so doing presents a tableau of America's national,
theological, and cultural promise. "The Piazza" undermines the unity
and fulfillment of the covenant between man and god that is implicit
in the picturesque. In treating MD, the study focuses on the epistemological basis of the novel's aesthetics, its cultural nationalism, the moral and horrific sublimity of its seascapes, the whale as
quintessential sublime, and its concluding vision of nature as
neither horrific nor redemptive. (DA: 37-3627)

See: Moore, Richard s. "Burke, Melville, and the 'Power of Blackness,'" American Transcendental Quarterly, 29: 30-33.

427. O'Brien, Ellen Joan. The Histrionic Vision: Dramatic and Theatrical Forms in the Novels of Herman Melville. Yale University, 1976. 245
pages. Order 77-14,296.

The histrionic device in characterization involves two categories:
the dramatic in which costume, action, and gesture or posture serve
as substantial links between appearance and reality and the theatrical (wherein these elements loose substance and become mere contri-
vances. Melville's darkening vision of the world is revealed in the
movement from the dramatic O to the theatrical CM. In O, R, and WJ,
costume serves as a vital means of self-expression. Taji and Pierre
are actor-heroes (protagonists featured in narrative passages that
are dramatic or approach drama) who fail in one way or another to
achieve self-dramatization. Ahab, however, succeeds in uniting self
and purpose. Costume dominates IP and CM, as it does in the earlier
works but the vision of reality conveyed here is one of "surface
projected not out of, but in the absence of, substance." (DA:
38-266)

428. Oravets, Andrew Joseph, Jr. Out of Kings: An Inquiry into the
Americanness of the Classic American Novel. Ohio State University, 1976.
169 pages. Order 76-18,018.

Americans have traditionally maintained an overblown sense of themselves, and this self-idealization of the country and its majority
has informed many of our great works of fiction. Ahab too eagerly
accepts his nation's Calvinistic assumptions and presses them to mon-
strous extremes. HM: 50-75. (DA: 37-972)

429. Pinker, Michael Joseph. The Sterne Voyage of the Pequod: the Tale
of a Tub in American Literature. SUNY-Binghampton, 1976. 229 pages.
Order 76-20,861.

The Tale of a Tub, "any kind of nonsense, fooling or absurdity" found in story form (either in content or in the telling), is traced from Aristophanes to Sterne whose sensibility and sentiment figure largely in America's literature. Melville's gift for open-ended tales and narrative chicanery especially in the later works is Shandean. The study concentrates on MD, its gamesome wordplay, Ishmael's logorrhea, and stylistic (if not direct) borrowings from Sterne. The novel's "great subject" is language, and it shows Melville to be "a great comedian at play." (DA: 37-1533)

430. Roundy, Nancy Louise. The Right Whale's Head and the Sperm Whale's Head: A Tension in Herman Melville's Work. University of Iowa, 1976. 204 pages. Order 76-26,324.

MD and P derive their epistemology and aesthetics from Plato and Coleridge's transcendental or "esemplastic" notion of the imagination, whereas PT and CM draw upon Locke's empiricism and Coleridge's "primary imagination." (DA: 37-2878)

See: Roundy, Nancy. "Fancies, Reflections and Things: The Imagination as Perception in 'The Piazza,'" College Language Association Journal, 20: 539-46. "Present Shadows: Epistemology in Melville's 'Benito Cereno,'" Arizona Quarterly, 34: 344-50. "'That is All I Know of Him': Epistemology and Art in Melville's 'Bartleby,'" Essays in Arts and Sciences, 9: 33-43. "Melville's The Confidence-Man: Epistemology and Art," Ball State University Forum, 21: 3-11.

431. Schunck, Ferdinand. The Poetry of Herman Melville. University of Bonn, 1976. 280 pages. (German).

Melville's theory of poetry as the synthesis of oppositions and of the poet as "the fusion of 'the largest heart with the largest brain'" has grounding in Renaissance, Coleridgean, Emersonian, and Arnoldian ideas. Throughout the poetry, works are structured upon dramatic and dialectic conflicts. Melville's abiltiy to "harmonize discordant formal features" even in his socially critical poems, attests to the once-intellectually tormented writer's achievement of "the serene wisdom of old age." (EASG, 1976, item 82)

See: Schunck, Ferdinand. Das Lyrische Werk Herman Melvilles. Bonn: Bouvier, 1976.

432. Stooke, David Edward. The Portrait of the Physician in Selected Prose Fiction of 19th Century American Authors. George Peabody College for Teachers, 1976. 151 pages. Order 77-3120.

The characterization of the physician in American fiction changes throughout the 19th century in accord with the progress of the medical profession. The study delineates six phases: primitive herb doctors, deluded scientist-doctors, esteemed general practitioners, village doctors, surgeons, and women doctors. O, WJ, and CM are briefly discussed. (DA: 37-5130)

433. Taylor, Kent Hewitt. Wittgenstein and Melville: A Study in the Character of Meaning. University of California at Santa Cruz, 1976. 221 pages. Order 77-16,800.

Interpretation should be a matter of connecting a text to external
referents. Language is a game, and meaning is best derived through
the examination of "linguistic encounters." Therefore, "when one
stays open to lines of linguistic connection, encounters which take
place in language ask one to find a linguistic place." Each text is a
unique "speaking" forth, and it must be interpreted in the immediacy
of that speaking. MD, P, CM, and BB, then, should be treated as
separate "beginnings" leading toward separate meanings. Each
requires its own approach. (DA: 38-793)

434. Toles, George Edward, Jr. The Darkening Window: Four Problematic
American Novels. University of Virginia, 1976. 211 pages. Order
76-22,880.

The problematic novel is the product of a stage in the author's mind
in which "contradictory impulses" are not resolved and adequate
vocabularies or imaginative constructs cannot be found to express the
conflict. Thus, the flaws of such a work communicate a meaning
concerning the failure of vision. The problem in P is that Melville
could not coordinate plot and prose style (he lacks here "an adequate
vocabulary of the heart) to shed light on the depths of his interior
being, a part of himself that he had come to see in the image of a
stone. HM: 53-105. (DA: 37-4378)

435. Wilmes, Douglas Robert.   The Satiric Mode in Melville's Fiction:
Pierre, Israel Potter, The Confidence-Man, and the Short Stories. University of Pennsylvania, 1976. 353 pages. Order 77-892.

Satire is not a genre but a mode or "style of perception and reaction
to experience" which first denies then reforms the reader's vision.
After a discussion of recent satiric theory (Alvin Kernan, in
particular), the study focuses on the problems of narrators as
"fictional satirists" and of characters as both satirists and
victims. Ultimately, satire need not rely upon "normalization" or
"historical particulars"; it is "an exercise in revelation." In P,
satire becomes an organic part of Melville's work, which becomes more
firmly entrenched in IP and CM. (DA: 37-4360)

1977

436. Adams, Karen Mary. Black Images in 19th Century American Painting
and Literature: An Iconological Study of Mount, Melville, Homer, and Mark
Twain. Emory University, 1977. 329 pages. Order 77-25,305.

The white man's images of the black man in painting and writing are
responses to white not black problems. Melville was fascinated with
the black man as an extension of the primitive mind and a reflection
of the deepest sectors of the inner self. Black figures and
cannibalism recur in MD. "Benito Cereno" employs painting-like
tableaux to puncture benign, racial stereotypes and show that all men
are slaves. After the Civil War (which diffused the power of the
Black man symbol), Melville created a white, black man (a blonde
barbarian) in BB. HM: 61-110. (DA: 38-7407)

437. Benensohn-Sager, Karen M. American Abrahams: Some Antinomian
Themes in American Literature. Northwestern University, 1977. 253 pages.
Order 78-5325.

Going beyond the myth of the American Adam, this study asserts that a
key theme in American literature is the myth of Abraham, or more
specifically, the problem of determining moral authority in the
context of an antinomian, Protestant culture. The works of Anne
Hutchinson, Kierkegaard, and Sartre provide the philosophical background. Antinomians respond to their problems of authority in one of
two modes: awareness of the risks of having no authority and ecstasy
in being free or above authorities. Neither Pierre nor Captain Vere
can escape the agony of their recognition that there are no "absolute
sources of value." HM: 158-222. (DA: 38-6719)

438. Bobb, Earl Victor. Education, the Protagonist, and the Nature of
Knowledge in Melville and Twain. University of Oregon, 1977. 209 pages.
Order 77-26,485.

The careers of Melville and Twain indicate the same pattern of
decline from one failed experiment in characterization to the next,
from light situations to despair. Within each of Melville's works
the same three-phase pattern of education occurs: 1) the protagonist's expectations are outlined, 2) preconceptions are destroyed,
and 3) a shocking or horrible revelation occurs. Taji, Redburn,
Ishmael, Pierre, Billy Budd, as well as characters in CM and the
tales are treated beside comparable works by Twain. (DA: 38-3495)

439. Bollas, Christopher Kim. Melville's Man: the Character of Breakdown. SUNY-Buffalo, 1977. 142 pages. Order 77-19,416.

Man's aesthetic experience has its origin in that moment in a
mother's care for her child when thought becomes "irrelevant to
survival." When the child grows, it internalizes both the mother and
this aesthetic moment; this internal self becomes the outward individual's "transformational other." An individual's action in the
world is a search for objects which will match the internalized
aesthetic moment or "other." Ishmael, Ahab, Pierre, and Bartleby are
manifestations of Melville's search for his "other." Pierre's
faltering vision of his mother turns back on himself, and in
"Bartleby" the lawyer and scrivener play the parts of outer and inner
selves. (DA: 38-1385)

See: Bollas, Christopher. "Melville's Lost Self: 'Bartleby,'"
American Imago, 31 (Winter 1974), 401-11.

440. Cahalan, James Fee. A Concordance to Melville's Moby-Dick. University of Pennsylvania, 1977. 1272 pages. Order 78-6562.

This computer generated list with a word frequency index is taken
from Feidelson's 1964 editon and provides generous contexts for all
words except a, an, by, of, to, and the. It shows Melville to have
used a highly diverse vocabulary (his ratio of word forms to running
words being 0.095 to 0.079). The Feidelson text was chosen over the
still unavailable Newberry/Northwestern edition because the former
had been computerized. A conversion table for the two texts is
forthcoming. (DA: 39-1561)

See: Cohen, Henning and James Cahalan, eds. A Concordance to Melville's Moby-Dick. 3 vols. Ann Arbor, Mi.: University Microfilms
International, 1978.

441. Connor, John Joseph. The Quixotic Novel from the Point of View of
the Narrative. University of Florida, 1977. 262 pages. Order 78-6684.

A structuralist analysis (a la Prapp and Barthes) of Don Quixote
reveals no single formula for the narrative, but rather a combination
of three kinds of narrative sequences (atomic, episodic, novelistic),
of which the latter two are more important. The episodic boils down
to an "abstract substratum" or formula $(Q \rightarrow V \rightarrow Q/V)$ in which the Don
(Q) attacks a victim (V) and becomes a victim himself (Q/V). The
novelistic narrative involves five subspecies (madness, psychology,
hero/fool, partners, self-conscious narrator). These "mobile fragments" pop up in subsequent novels, including MD. Ahab, for
instance, follows the formula of the victimized victimizer (q.v.).
HM: 198-249. (DA: 38-6700)

442. Connor, Marian. The Abysm and the Star: A Study of the Poetry of
Herman Melville. Boston University, 1977. 214 pages. Order 77-21,583.

This reading of the poems focuses on two conflicting tendencies:
Melville's attraction for the real or actual and his inclination to
speculate on objects or events. Melville's "epigrammatic poems,"
though relatively few in number, adhere to the former principle while
John Marr demonstrates the latter. Also treated are BP (which
reveals a variety of stances) and Clarel (which is an ambitious
attempt to resolve the various stances it poses). (DA: 38-2122)

443. Dellavedova, Benjamin Robert. The Carnivorous Words: A Study in
Herman Melville. University of Tulsa, 1977. 115 pagse. Order 77-18,737.

Melville abandoned fiction because he came to realize that all
written forms deceive readers. To give the lie to fiction, the
author employed two devices: the "fabulated man" or character who
represents an institution or its documents and "documental fabula-
tion" or written forms that represent an event. Bartleby's association with documents makes him an example of the former, and the
conclusion of "Benito Cereno" demonstrates the latter. (DA: 38-1386)

444. Dyer, Susan Athearn. Plinlimmon's Theme: The Aspirations and Limitations of Man in the Novels of Herman Melville. Duke University, 1977.
223 pages. Order 77-31,664.

Plinlimmon's pamphlet is taken as the moral center in P, and the
Horological/Chronometrical dialectic is pursued throughout the canon.
A sense of timelessness pervades T, O, and M providing "glimpses of
eternity" that prefigure Plinlimmon. (The theme also occurs in various works by Hawthorne which may have influenced Melville.) Ana-
logues for "Ei" appear in MD, hinting that perhaps the pamphlet was
written during the composition of MD. The cosmopolitan proves to be
innocent of any wrong-doing in a novel which admits of "the possibility for horological resolution in ... [a] fallen world." Finally,
the Plinlimmon theme is re-examined in the light of psychoanalytic
theory. (DA: 38-4824)

445. Ferguson, Terrance John. "The Test of Greatness": The Grotesque in Melville's Major Novels. University of Toronto, 1977. 389 pages.

The "grotesque" derives from a vision of defeat and of "man as a victim of his encounter with the demonic," and its structure is one of transformation or metamorphosis. The grotesque vision exceeds the tragic in that its terror has no end or release. Finally, laughter accompanies the grotesque "triumph of the demonic." Melville's major works pass through three stages of grotesque characterization: the comic (M), the tragic (MD, P), and the satiric (CM). (DA: 39-2271)

446. Hanson, Elizabeth I. The Indian Metaphor in the American Renaissance. University of Pennsylvania, 1977. 288 pages. Order 77-19,858.

America's violent, colonial, and expansionist impulses provide a context for the evolving image of the Indian. While Parkman and Greeley saw the American primitive as either childish or deserving of annihilation, artists such as Melville created Indian figures which in their resemblance to the white man were both compassionate and savage. In his representations of white man/Indian relations, Melville bodies forth the hope for and complexities of a rapprochement between the two. In the process, his ambiguous use of metaphor urges us away from easy misconceptions and self-deception. (DA: 38-1388)

See: Hanson, Elizabeth I. "Melville and the Polynesian-Indian," Melville Society Extracts, 17 (February 1974), 13-4.

447. Harris, Susan Kumin. Invisible Spheres: The Rhetorical Response to the Loss of Moral Certainty in Herman Melville and Mark Twain. Cornell University, 1977. 275 pages. Order 78-7782.

Rhetoric reflects a moral vision, and artists strive to fashion their rhetoric in such a way as to make that moral vision coherent. Both Melville and Twain suffer a breakdown in moral vision which affected their rhetorical structures. While MD exhibits consistent language, harmonious compositions, and a clear vision, P indicates a collapse and BB a reversal of that vision. Once a believer in the divinity of mass man, Melville comes to see men in the mass as a mob. Ultimately, Melville escapes nihilism but at the expense of adopting "a narrow, authoritarian vision of man and society." (DA: 38-7332)

448. Holden, Sarah Halland. Changes in the Novel: A Structuralist Comparison of Middlemarch, The Confidence-Man, and Absalom, Absalom! Rice University, 1977. 181 pages. Order 77-19,264.

For the most part, 19th century fiction uses an omniscient narrator speaking in clear language to convey a clear moral concern. The reader sits and listens. Twentieth century narrative techniques call the narrator's reliability into question and engage the reader in a search for meaning embodied in a language that is intentionally multi-interpretational. CM is a transitional novel in that its narrative technique is traditional but its use of language and its muddy vision resemble 20th century novels. (DA: 38-1409)

449. Kellner, Robert Scott. <u>Toads and Scorpions: Women and Sex in the</u>
<u>Writings of Melville</u>. University of Massachusetts, 1977. 217 pages.
Order 77-22,023.

Love in America is characterized either as civilizing or destructive.
Melville's treatment of women invariably follows the latter. As "the
Yillah-Hautia figure" draws upon Fayaway, so does the germinal theme
of sex and death in T come to function in M. P culminates Melville's
view of women as sexually irresistable and destructive. Women are
central in the words not as heroines but as forces which motivate the
hero to action. (<u>DA</u>:¯38-2127)

See: Kellner, Robert. "Sex, Toads, and Scorpions: A Study of the
Psychological Themes in Melville's <u>Pierre</u>," <u>Arizona Quarterly</u>, 31:
5-19.

450. Langston, David James. <u>Mediation and Interpretation: An Inquiry</u>
<u>into Romantic Ways of Knowing</u>. Stanford University, 1977. 326 pages.
Order 77-25,692.

The cognitive role of interpretation in Romanticism takes on two
shapes. Signs may be clear emblems of meaning meant to elevate the
perceiver into a transcendent state of being in which both mind and
object (perceiver and perceived) unite and lose or share identity.
This "two term romanticism" gives way to "three term romanticism"
when the perceiver becomes conscious that the sign is itself a sign.
Meaning, then, becomes a matter of the perceiver's interpretation of
the "opaque" sign within a cultural context and with respect to
shared habits of thought and behavior. Melville is a "three term"
romantic, and this study explores <u>MD</u>, <u>CM</u>, and <u>BB</u> to determine "how
Melville dramatizes the problem of shared knowledge." HM: 159-285.
(<u>DA</u>: 38-3469)

451. Limprecht, Nancy Silverman. <u>Repudiating the Self-Justifying</u>
<u>Fiction: Charles Brockden Brown, Nathaniel Hawthorne, and Herman Melville</u>
<u>as Anti-Romancers</u>. University of California at Berkeley, 1977. 601
pages. Order 78-12,659.

Romance is a comforting form of wish-fulfillment seeking to reinforce
the reader's understanding of the world and self. Critics of the
18th and 19th centuries, by and large, castigated the self-indulgent
form and encouraged a form of realism that gave "rise to the novel."
Yet some critics allowed that moral fiction could as well be a
working out of the artist's fears and desires rather than a representation of an objective reality, and a handful of artists stayed
with the Romance but inverted its features so as to demonstrate deep
truths while denying the viability of either romance or novel. They
wrote, then, "self-justifying fictions" or "anti-romances." T, for
instance, is a bit of "romancing" because it is a psychological
justification of the author's real life retreat from an return to
civilization. HM: 392-559. (<u>DA</u>: 39-886)

452. Lincoln, Jerry Joseph. <u>The Dream as a Metaphor for Altered States</u>
<u>of Consciousness in the Fiction of Poe, Hawthorne, and Melville</u>.
University of Chicago, 1977. 377 pages.

Dreams fall into two traditions: skeptical and assertive. On the
one hand, they are enigmatic and expressive of the "variety of
earthly life." On the other, they may be sources for knowledge of
self and the world. Both traditions develop throughout English
literature, and both conceptions occur in the intellectual milieu of
early 19th century America. Dream elicits both wonder and symbolism,
and in Melville's case it serves as a metaphor for consciousness
which suggests an ambivalent approach to both dream traditions.
Dreams for Pierre may be false or incomplete; for Ishmael they are an
avenue of insight (although only one of many avenues.) HM: 265-364.

453. Lofgren, Hans Borje. Democratic Skepticism: Literary-Historical
Point of View in Cooper, Hawthorne, and Melville. University of
California at Santa Cruz, 1977. 281 pages. Order 78-4539.

"Democratic Skepticism" in various American authors is a point of
view that can be analyzed in terms of the author's attitude toward
society and toward his fictional subject. Melville, for instance,
projects a sense of alienation through an aristocratic rhetoric
directed toward a democratic subject. WJ is the point upon which
Melville pivots (with nudges from Hawthorne) from democratic idealism
to skepticism. In attempting to suggest a democratization of the
Navy, he hints darkly at the inherent tyranny in men. MD shows that
freedom itself does not exist. HM: 165-245. (DA: 38-6714)

454. Lojek, Helen Heusner. Ministers and Their Sermons in American
Literature. University of Denver, 1977. 292 pages. Order 77-17,183.

Fictional depictions of the minister in the 19th century generally
center upon the epistemological conflict over how one can know God's
will. Ministers of the heart preach emotional routes; those of the
head, the rational. Viewed in the context in which it appears,
Father Mapple's Sermon presents "a point of view," a highly personal
interpretation, but only one of many interpretations. HM: 11-35.
(DA: 38-787)

455. McCort, Thomas Michael. Fate and Foreknowledge: Necessity and
Prophecy in Melville's Fiction. University of Michigan, 1977. 258 pages.
Order 77-18,075.

"Determinism" involves both "predestination" (a scriptural doctrine)
and "philosophical necessity" (an aspect of the rationalist theory of
causality). Prophecy, a natural adjunct of determinism, was accordingly a matter of divine revelation or a foretelling of effects by a
study of causes. Both determinism and prophecy had considerable play
in Melville's time, and as his literary career progressed from M to
the tales, his works incorporated the concept of philosophical necessity to the fullest while the notion of prophecy after P declines.
BB, too, reflects the trends in social determinism of the latter half
of the century. (DA: 38-1391)

456. Mushabac, Jane. Humor in Melville. CUNY, 1977. 299 pages. Order
77-14,588.

"Humorous prose," contrary to the standard function of prose, debunks
authority and celibrates man (over God) as "an all powerful explorer

of the universe." Three humorous prose traditions (Renaissance, amiable, and American frontier humor) fuse in Melville's own brand of humor. After examining humorists in these traditions that Melville read or was likely to have read, the study shows that Melville strives in the first five novels to find "full ranging" humorous voices, which he discovers in MD. The element of expansiveness in the humor succeeds in the later fiction with the notable exceptions of P and BB. (DA: 38-266)

See: Mushabac, Jane. Humor in Melville. New York: Archon, 1982.

457. Pancost, David William. Washington Irving's Sketch Book and American Literature to the Rise of Realism: Framed Narrative, the Pictorial Mode, and Irony in the Fiction of Irving, Longfellow, Kennedy, Poe, Hawthorne, Melville, Howells, Twain, James, and Others. Duke University, 1977. 356 pages. Order 78-7619.

The framing of various sketches in one book suggests two characteristics: pictorialism (since the tales are framed like pictures) and irony (since the framing creates distance between author and reader). Although Irving's own skill in fashioning works that could match The Sketch Book failed, other practitioners (notably Poe and Hawthorne) succeeded. Melville's foray occurs at a time when the sketch book form gave way to periodical publication and realism. PT and especially "The Encantadas" are "an uncompromising attack on the pictorial mode and romantic idealism." HM: 272-80. (DA: 38-7336)

See: Pancost, David W. "Donald Grant Mitchell's Reveries of a Bachelor and Herman Melville's 'I and My Chimney,'" American Transcendental Quarterly, 42 (1979): 129-36.

458. Quirk, Thomas Vaughan. The Confidence-Man: Melville's Problem of Faith. University of New Mexico, 1977. 164 pages. Order 77-27,179.

Understanding what the cosmopolitan is up to will allow us to understand the novel as a whole. In his many disguises, he is a satiric device that attacks both the deceptive and gullible elements of society. That the novel is "infidel," overly dark, or devil-ridden is a misreading that places undue emphasis on the first half (which satirizes dishonesty). The interpolated tales and authorial intrusions provide a means by which we may discern a positive structure--especially in the cosmopolitan who in his "originality" most closely resembles Don Quixote. Ultimately, the work is more of an "anatomy of faith" than a novel. (DA: 38-3503)

See: Quirk, Tom. "Saint Paul's Types of the Faithful and Melville's Confidence-Man," Nineteenth Century Fiction, 28 (1974), 472-7. "Two Sources in The Confidence-Man," Melville Society Extracts, 39: 12-14. "Man Traps and Melville," Melville Society Extracts, 44: 11-12. Melville's Confidence Man: From Knave to Knight. Columbia, Mo.: University of Missouri Press, 1982.

459. Ramsey, William McCrea. The Confidence-Man: Melville and the Reader. University of North Carolina at Chapel Hill, 1977. 366 pages. Order 78-7156.

Melville's last novel is a "self consuming artifact" in that its style and characterization contrive against the reader to subvert his aesthetic assumptions. It is as well a "comic burlesque of novelistic technique." Also, each narrative sequence pits the myths of the Passion and of the Fall against each other to create a burlesque of communion that indicates the reader's "own fall from innocence." (DA: 38-7336)

See: Ramsey, William M. "Melville's and Barnum's Man with a Weed," American Literature, 51: 101-4. "'Touching' Scenes in The Confidence-Man," Emerson Society Quarterly, 25: 37-42. "The Moot Points of Melville's Indian-Hating," American Literature, 52 (May 1980), 224-235.

460. Richardson, Nancy Lee. Melville's Attitude Toward America. University of Delaware, 1977. 276 pages. Order 77-20,556.

While Melville's fellow Americans believed in a three-part doctrine of faith in democracy (that democracy is a consequence of nature, that the democrat is free and responsible, and that the nation's destiny was to expand democracy), Melville challenged these principles (despite his own patriotic background), arguing throughout his works, that many political alternatives exist for all peoples. As for America, itself, he grew to believe that the New World was not a corrective for the Old World ills but just another "accomplice in the moral guilt of all civilization." The early novels, M in particular, introduced political problems that are heightened in MD. Here, Melville exposes the nation's self-contradictory stance of commercialism and utopianism. CM is a mature satire and BB calls for a return to the tradition of established law to preserve an "individual's natural sovreignty." (DA: 38-2129)

461. Rothmayr, Ludwig. Man and Fate in Herman Melville: An Investigation of the Development of the Idea of Destiny in His Novels. University of Regensburg, 1977. 315 pages. (German).

From T to BB, Melville's works reveal a pattern of action that proves the author to be "a convinced determinist." Once man's vision of a balance between nature and supernature fails, his own identity falters. He fights the antagonistic universe but ultimately resigns. (EASG, 1977, item 98)

See: Rothmayr, Ludwig. Der Mensch und das Schicksal in den Romanen Herman Melvilles (Regensburger Arbeiten zur Anglistik un Amerikanistik 10), Frankfort: Lang, 1977.

462. Siegel, Mark Andrew. Dialectics of Consciousness: Melville and the Realistic Imagination. Rutgers University, 1977. 246 pages. Order 77-25,019.

Resisting the temptation to recast Melville in our own likeness as a modernist, the study proposes (contra Guetti and Edgar Dryden) that Melville's literary aesthetics is a dialectic between realism (the impulse toward representational art) and modernism (the impulse toward self-referential and self-destructive art). T and O come closest to Melville's understanding of Balzac's realism, but the last section of M initiates patterns of modernism. From MD on, each work exhibits a clash between both traditions and their incumbent notions of ordered and disordered worlds. (DA: 38-2796)

463. Silverman, Jay Ross. The Destruction of the Primitive: A Study of Melville. University of Virginia, 1977. 188 pages. Order 78-12,097.

Because Melville invariably presents the primitive through the eyes of a civilized man, primitivism is a reflection of the civilized sensibility, a complex of psychological, cognitive and economic factors. Generally speaking, Melville began as a "radical Rousseauist" with respect to primitivism, but toward the end of his career, he came to be more conservative, a "Hobbesean" recognizing that man's primitive impulses must be controlled. T mediates the primitive and civilized. MD, as a novel concerned with an economic quest, reveals the psychological and primitive underpinnings of industrialism. The later fiction emphasized the horror of the primitive, and in BB we find the last vestige of a positive primitivism "on the edge of forfeiture." (DA: 39-888)

464. Simpson, Judy Aycock. Herman Melville's Battle-Pieces and Aspects of the War: Background, Structure, and Meaning. Memorial University of Newfoundland, 1977. 272 pages.

In view of Melville's notion of the social function of poetry, and his architectonics and organic theories of composition, BP is clearly a "unified volume of poetry." The collection also reveals three facets of Melville's life: patriot, citizen, and philosopher-poet. (DA: 39-7349)

465. Wander, John Michael. Cries to the Wilderness: Melville, Hopkins, Eliot. SUNY-Stony brook, 1977. 320 pages. Order 77-25,357.

Art is both "the product of a human being trammeled with concerns" and a guide to his understanding of the "destructive, redemptive processes of life." Melville's art performs this function with respect to the 19th century problem of the de-mythification of nature and the dissolution of faith. CM explores this "environment." HM: 1-106. (DA: 38-3461)

466. Wright, John Samuel. Ethiopia in Babylon: Antebellum American Romanticism and the Emergence of Black Literary Nationalism. University of Minnesota, 1977. 500 pages. Order 77-26,179.

Brief mention is given to "Benito Cereno" as a fictional account of a slave uprising in this extensive study of race and literature. The tale is the only work in its period to manipulate the symbols of racism. HM: 194-98. (DA: 38-3506)

467. Zoellner, Alan Frederick. The Splendid Labyrinth: Language, Consciousness, and the Contraries in Melville's Later Fiction. Indiana University, 1977. 291 pages. Order 78-5646.

Melville's works are a response to the Emersonian notion of language as the principal avenue of transcendence. The early novels up to MD concur with the ideal precept; the later fiction, however, reacts against it, revealing Melville's "skepticism about the power of language." In contrast to Emerson's image of the poet as an "Ichor drinker," Melville in the later works present the poet as a digger in the quarries of "his own mysterious being." Melville displays these "psychic labyrinths" most effectively in P, CM, and BB. (DA: 38-11)

1978

468. Baurecht, William Carl. Romantic Deviance and the Messianic Impulse in American Masculinity: Case Studies of Moby-Dick, One Flew over the Cuckoo's Nest, and Sometimes a Great Notion. University of New Mexico, 1978. 399 pages. Order 79-12,928.

Through Ahab, Ishmael, and Queequeg, Melville abandons the traditional precepts of the "male myth" and concludes that American manhood is a factor which "the mind must delimit amid shifting illusions." HM: 100-182. (DA: 39-7343)

469. Burns, Mandy Schreiber. Crisis of Confidence: A Study of the Confidence Man as a Metaphor in Melville's Novels. Claremont Graduate School, 1978. 192 pages. Order 78-14,829.

The best place to find sources for the confidence man figure is in Melville's own works. In T and O, Melville recognizes that he must wear various masks in order to body forth a world that is itself composed of masks. His decision to paint Long Ghost as a morally controlled trickster indicates the cheerfulness with which Melville adopts the concept. Taji's masking, however, is an act of self deception (rather than Long-Ghost's self-awareness), a fact which reflects harshly upon the author's shape-shifting potential. Redburn, White Jacket, and Ishmael reaffirm the possibility of the artist and man holding on to faith, but Ahab is an "imposter" informing us of the "impossibility of faith." P and CM present Melville's last confidence men who explore those problems of faith that both "encourage and ... frustrate both writer and reader. (DA: 39-1561)

470. Cavanaugh, Miriam Katharine. The Romantic Hero in Byron, Hawthorne, and Melville. University of Massachusetts, 1978. 270 pages. Order 78-16,243.

The Byronic hero (or "gloomy egoist in an alien universe) is the pattern for Melville's protagonist in M, MD, and P. Taji and Pierre are particularly vexed in that, unlike Ahab, they cannnot in their encounters with themselves, their women, and societies clearly discern good from evil. HM: 109-72. (DA: 39-1563)

471. Davis, David G. The Image of the Minister in American Fiction. University of Tulsa, 1978. 178 pages. Order 78-12,308.

American authors have protrayed ministers in a variety of ways. Brief mention is given to Father Mapple, a strong and dignified soul, and Falsgrave who is "most repugnant." (DA: 39-882)

472. Dettlaf, Shirley M. Hebraism and Hellenism in Melville's Clarel:
The Influence of Arnold, Goethe, and Schiller. University of Southern
California, 1978. 220 pages.

Melville's poetry and marginalia (especially his reading of early
German Romantics and Arnold) provide clues to Melville's aesthetics.
Closely compared are Arnold, Melville's notion of Arnold's Hebraic-
Hellenic split, and Clarel. While the long poem reveals that Melville
departs from Arnold on religion and (in part) on art, it attempts an
Arnoldian synthesis of the impulses to dive and to restrain. But the
study concludes that the Hebraic element is strong enough in Melville's work to make the two concepts a "dichotomy" rather than "synthesis." (DA: 39-2910)

See: Dettlaff, Shirley M. "Ionian Form and Essau's Waste:
Melville's View of Art in Clarel," Melville Society Extracts, 41: 2,
and American Literature, 54 (May 1982), 212-228.

473. Elias, Mohamed. The India of Melville and Mark Twain: A Study in
Geo-Cultural Symbolism. University of Kerala (India), 1978. 412 pages.

For Americans the passage to India was a figurative instance of their
expansion, politically and psychologically, in the unknown. For Melville, the image of India has literal applications as well. His use
of the mandala, the concept of the avatar, and the wisdom of the
moghul can be found in M, R, and MD. Patterns of India imagery found
in Clarel reinforce those in the fiction.

474. Gidmark, Jill Barnum. Melville's Sea Vocabulary: A Commentary and
a Glossed Concordance. University of North Dakota, 1978. 699 pages.
Order 79-4704.

Melville drew his sea vocabulary more from his own experience than
his reading. Throughout the first six works, he uses 345 separate
lexical units relating to the sea, mostly in noun form but also in
imaginative compounds. His sea vocabulary and word-compounding
increase from novel to novel with noticeable peaks in M and MD. The
words fall into four types; those referring to 1) the sea proper, 2)
land-sea junctures, 3) animate and inanimate but non-human associations, and 4) human roles. Introductory chapters discuss the frequency, distribution, and metaphoric use of the terms. Appendices
list the vocabulary alphabetically, by semantic group, and syntactic
classification; word compounds and metaphoric activity are also
listed by novel. Entries in the list itself provide etymologies and
definitions from dictionaries used in Melville's time and the present. Contexts for each appearance of each word are included with
page references to the Newberry-Northwestern texts and to the Hay-
ford-Parker edition of MD. (DA: 39-5511)

See: Gidmark, Jill B. Melville's Sea Dictionary: A Glossed
Concordance and Analysis of The Sea Language in Melville's Nautical
Novels. Westport, Conn.: Greenwood Press, 1982.

475. Greenberg, Robert M. Chasing the Leviathan: Religious and Philoso-
phic Uncertainty in Moby-Dick. CUNY, 1978. 192 pages. Order 78-16,680.

The problem of philosophical uncertainty may be seen from two vantage
points: nature as an object and nature subjectively perceived.
While MD vacillates between these world views, it shows that the
"outward life--dramatic and vigorous, even heroic--dominates."
Separate chapters treat Ahab (the novel's center), Ishmael, Queequeg,
narrative problems, Cetology (both as philosophy and comedy), and the
last three chapters. (DA: 39-1566)

476. Kosinski, Mark Kermit. American Culture As System: A Methodologi-
cal Inquiry. Bowling Green State University, 1978. 178 pages. Order
78-19,861.

In trying to meet the need for a structuralist approach to the
American studies movement, this study offers a semiological model for
culture and applies it to MD. In brief, a sign system groups
together a number of cognitive and sociological principles of structure which are the "code" for the culture. The advantages of the
approach are that it is non-ideological, ahistorical, and culturally
comprehensive. Ishmael is a "semiotic adventurer," because he
searches for order through sign making, but his codes are not internal constraints; they manifest the diverse codes of his culture. HM:
121-50. (DA: 39-3004)

477. Moses, Carole Horsburgh. Like Race to Run: Melville's Use of
Spenser. SUNY-Binghampton, 1978. 260 pages. Order 78-7108.

Melville's marginalia in his five volume set of Spenser indicate his
understanding of the poet's dual vision of spiritual achievement and
thwarted quests. While Spenser separates good from evil and
perceives cosmic unity in harsh reality, Melville selected, inverted,
and at times seemingly misapprehended Spenser's images in order to
convey his own doubts. As Melville's vision darkened, he dropped his
references to Spenser altogether. Works treated include T, M, MD, P,
the tales, CM, and Clarel. (DA: 38-7335)

See: Moses, Carole. "Melville's Use of Spenser in 'The Piazza.'"
College Language Association Journal, 20: 222-31.

478. Nelson, James Andrew. Herman Melville's Use of the Bible in Billy
Budd. University of Iowa, 1978. 213 pages. Order 79-2926.

A review of BB criticism and a chapter listing Old and New Testament
allusions in the novel precede a discussion of Melville's careful use
of the Bible. Following Wayne Booth's suggestions in The Rhetoric of
Irony, the study determines that many biblical allusions are ironic
and that Melville's emphasis upon the Old Testament reinforces a
reading of the work that makes Billy an Adamic figure and God "the
envious marplot of Eden." (DA: 39-4987)

479. Ra'ad, Basem Lutfi. Melville's Landscape in Clarel. University of
Toronto, 1978. 226 pages.

Melville's use of "natural and created landscapes" is the basis for
this study of the author's aesthetics, philosophy, and religion.

Images of man-made artifacts appearing in natural settings serve as
crucial links to our understanding of the religious development in
the poem; they also indicate Melville's increasing concern for
objectivism in his aesthetics. The study examines the Journal as
well as the function of landscape in the poem's sequential deaths,
the problem of myth, and the use of such images as rocks, rainbows,
and palms. (DA: 39-4260)

480. Rosner, Mary I. Novel Beginnings: A Rhetorical Analysis of
Overtures in 19th Century Fiction. Ohio State University, 1978. 189
pages. Order 78-12,380.

Prefaces, preludes, apologies, introductions, front matter: they all
introduce novels, but they are functional too in that they begin to
shape the reader's expectatins of things to come. The study arranges
six novels (four British, two American) in order of the increasing
degree to which the reader is responsible for making sense of what he
is about to read. "Etymology" and "Extracts" in MD force the reader
to question both the narrator and himself and to see the shortcomings
of literary conventions. HM: 132-56. (DA: 39-903)

481. Sackmary, Regina Joyce. Horizons of the Self: Autobiography and
First-Person Narrative in Early American Literature. CUNY, 1978. 259
pages. Order 78-16,702.

Discovering the relationship of the self to society was a fundamental
concern of Puritan and early-Republic Americans. The use of the
first-person narrative was indigenous to this concern, for it records
an individual's "crisis of self-definition," both personally and with
respect to the nation's emerging consciousness. Thus, this and the
organic autobiographical mode are a means of establishing the "confidence of identity." Like Hawthorne, Melville (treated with Poe) is a
romantic who transforms the personal narrative from its optimistic
beginnings to a deeper interior autobiographical fiction. HM:
204-36. (DA: 39-1576)

482. Salomon, Amy. Melville's Mardi: and A Voyage Thither: A Study in
Political Philosophy. New School for Social Research, 1978. 212 pages.
Order 79-8646.

Merrell Davis saw M as a "chartless voyage" composed of three
separate works (realistic, allegorical, and political). This study,
however, argues that the "riddle" of M's structure can be cracked by
seeing the work as joining together three voyages (for Sperm Whale,
for land, and for Yillah) each of which prepares the reader for the
next and points toward the "eternal goal" of the West. The novel's
structure also finds unity in the inter-relationship of Truth and
Eros, a conflict which is resolved in Serenia where love and faith
dominate. (DA: 39-6316)

483. Sattin, Jerry Paul. Allegory in Modern Fiction: A Study of
Moby-Dick, The Brothers Karamazov, and "Die Verwandlung." University of
Illinois at Champaign, 1978. 265 pages. Order 78-11,288.

This study argues for an acceptance of allegory as a fluid form, not
one in which word and idea are rigidly wedded but one in which the

narrative bodies forth meaning or even myth. As allegory, MD
presents problems with the traditional notion of the form, for
allegories should not be so ambiguous. But in fact, allegory often
deliberately veils or cloaks its meaning. MD, in effect, is a number
of allegories stemming from each of the novel's principal
allegorists: Ahab, Starbuck, and Ishmael. The novel's final
ambiguity lies in the problem of which of these allegories is, in
fact, Melville's. HM: 64-125. (DA: 39-272)

484. Shanahan, Daniel Augustus. Narcissus Judged: The Decline of Individualism in Fiction since 1850; Studies in Melville, Conrad, Joyce, and
Dostoevsky. Stanford University, 1978. 232 pages. Order 78-22,571.

Man has outgrown that form of individualism in which one may expect
to find moral and philosophical truths revealed by an "inner voice."
Beginning with a discussion of the contrasting views of the
individual as embodied in Nietzsche and Freud, this study examines
the path now being cut in our culture that will take us "beyond
individualism" to a comprehension of "otherness." In modern fiction,
irony is the tool which allows us to indict and judge characters and
their individualism. With Ishmael counterbalancing Ahab, Melville
was able to distil the essence of the conflict between individualism
and its other-directed opposite. HM: 105-31. (DA: 39-3575)

485. Sundquist, Eric John. Home As Found: Authority and Genealogy in
Cooper, Thoreau, Hawthorne, and Melville. Johns Hopkins University, 1978.
495 pages. Order 78-17,977.

The family is the author's surrogate for "a past." The desire for or
oppression of the family indicates the degree to which the author is
dependent upon such a model for social and political power. Authority (both in the paternal and literary sense), then, is at issue
here, and Freud's "family romance" as epitomized in the totemic meal
situation is a further route for the investigation of genealogy and
American literature. P embodies "a true American Hamletism, a point
of crisis figuring authority at an impotent crossroads where the
struggle is so internalized that it can generate only a wild, self-
reflexive parody." HM: 321-420. (DA: 39-2279)

See: Sundquist, Eric. Home As Found: Authority and Genealogy in
Nineteenth-Century American Literature. Baltimore, Md.: Johns
Hopkins University Press, 1979.

486. Thomson, Jean Basehore. Imagery as Language in Melville's Mardi and
Moby-Dick. University of Iowa, 1978. 278 pages. Order 79-12,909.

Language itself is an image; therefore a close look at linguistics
will help elucidate Melville's writings, in particular M and MD, the
image patterns of which are extensive. The study examines feature
transfers in Melville's metaphors as well as patterns in sentences,
paragraphs and chapters. It also discusses the problem of wrestling
meaning out of images. (DA: 39-7349)

487. Wegener, Larry Edward. A Concordance to Herman Melville's Clarel:
A Poem and Pilgrimage to the Holy Land. University of Nebraska at
Lincoln, 1978. 886 pages. Order 79-16,463.

The concordance uses the first American edition as text (the same
designated as copy text for the proposed Newberry-Northwestern
edition) and supplies complete line contexts as well as Part-Canto-
line references for most words in Melville's 18,217 line poem.
Appendices gather together Melville's corrections of the Putnam
edition, capitalized words, phrases, pronouns, words used in simile
(as, like, than, etc.), and section titles. A list of deleted words
(including I and me) and their frequencies appear in the
Introduction. (DA: 40-260)

See: Wegener, Larry Edward, ed. A Concordance to Herman Melville's
Clarel: A Poem and Pilgrimage in the Holy Land. Glassboro, N.J.:
Melville Society, 1979.

                              1979

488. Alexandrov, Vladimir E. Cognition and National Destiny in the Major
Novels of Herman Melville and Andrej Belyj. Princeton University (Comparative Literature), 1979. 422 pages. Order 79-18,547.

Although Melville and Andrej Belyj are symbolists who could not have
influenced each other, their approach to epistemology and their conception of their countries' futures make them kindred souls. Both
artists are discussed in terms of "flux" and "rigidity." Whereas
Melville felt that only "fluxional" modes of cognition were suited
for survival, America was heading toward a "rigid" epistemology; thus
the failures of such rigid thinkers as Ahab and Pierre are a cautionary example for the nation. Symbols of flux in MD are sea voyaging
and water gazing (as opposed to the rigid land); and in P the hero
sees "fluidity as a damning ambiguity." HM: 8-144, 317-402. (DA:
40-834)

489. Antoine, Shannon Louise. Melville and the Art of Satire: Perspect-
tive through Parody and Caricature. Louisiana State University, 1979.
315 pages. Order 79-21,953.

Satire appears in portions of all the works and even dominates the
structuring of M, P, and CM. In the early works, Melville focuses on
the traditional topics of satire (social and cultural abuses, politics, false gods, hypocrisy), but as his works become more satiric,
he relied more upon techniques of "indirection." The self-
conscious "fictiveness" of CM, for instance, forces the reader into
active interpretation; and to this satiric end, Melville employed,
most effectively, "parody" and "caricature." Both forms engage the
reader in that they require us to compare the fictive satire to an
original. In the early works, Melville parodies objects and texts in
the objective world and in history; in the later fiction, his objects
are created within the fictional structure itself. (That is, M
parodies real people but Plinlimmon in P parodies Pierre himself.)
The three double tales also demonstrate this latter day parodic
technique. (DA: 40-2058)

490. Atlas, Marilyn Judith. A Psychobiographical Approach to Moby-Dick. Michigan State University, 1979. 198 pages. Order 79-21,131.

Where Melville's relationship with Hawthorne failed because Melville attempted "a fully reciprocal," absolutist friendship with a shy man not yet ready for such an involvement, his novel MD succeeds in bodying forth a sense of fluidity lacking in Melville's personal experience. Specifically, Melville was able to transfer the frustrations and emotions invested in the friendship into the metaphor and characters in MD. The images of the line and circle, favored by Melville because of their "mystical transcendence and cold, unrelenting destruction," are supremely adaptable to the author's need for fluid expression. (Lines become circles; circles bisect lines). By refusing to sanction the different solutions to the human condition offered by Ahab, Starbuck and Ishmael, Melville also preserves the novel's "creative resistance of absolutes." (DA: 40-1463)

491. Black, Ronald James. The Paradoxical Structure of the Sea Quest in Dana, Poe, Cooper, Melville, London, and Hemingway. Wayne State University, 1979. 300 pages. Order 80-10,123.

In response to the well-known lack of "literary material" in American life, American writers have written works which play upon the tension between society and nature. But whereas explorations into the wilderness often involve idealized notions of nature which rejuvenate the wanderer, sea fiction bodies forth a more alien version of nature through a series of paradoxes: self discovery and annihilation, freedom and imprisonment, unity and alienation. Melville's mariners synthesize these in various dialectical modes of the sea quest. Tommo endures an incomplete synthesis in his attempts to find an ideal world; Redburn, too, cannot resolve the problems of "growth and destruction" incumbent upon initiation. Ishmael anguishes through his self discovery amidst a world void of meaning, whereas the narrator in BB resolves the paradox. HM: 206-53. (DA: 40-5862)

492. Cheikin, Miriam Quen. Billy Budd or, the Ambiguities. CUNY, 1979. 211 pages. Order 79-23,711.

Critics have too frequently judged BB, a product of the 19th century, from a 20th century perspective. Seen in its proper historical setting and within the development of Melville's canon, the novel is less redemptive, more bitter, than most would admit. "Circumstantial evidence" taken from the author's milieu (his tendency in the later years and works to criticize those "who [rely] on custom, form or law to mandate their decisions" and his concern over outliving his two sons) support the "testament of resistance" approach to the novel which condemns Vere. (DA: 40-2670)

See: Cheikin, Miriam Quen. "Captain Vere: Darkness Made Visible," Arizona Quarterly, 34: 293-310.

493. Clouser, Marcia Ann McMullen. Mystic Gestures: Herman Melville's Images of the Body. University of Texas at Austin, 1979. 504 pages. Order 80-9842.

Melville uses bodily gestures in his fiction as symbols and devices for characterization and plot. In general, his characters are

"activists," but early on they tend to be inept. Their awkward
descents, ascents, and drownings artfully body forth their problematic mental journeys. Queequeg and Ishmael, however, are practiced
divers. Their "kinetic" gesture is resurrection. (DA: 40-5864)

494. Gilliland, Joe Drake. Herman Melville's Portraits of the Artist.
Arizona State University, 1979. 276 pages. Order 79-19,175.

Melville's review of Hawthorne's Mosses reveals that art must plunge
beneath the surface of things to find truth. To convey this, Melville fashioned his questing protagonists in the mold of the artist.
The early artist-heroes, while not strictly artists, are nevertheless
storytellers conscious of Melville's aesthetics. The tragic trilogy
of M, MD, and P details the artist's movement toward nihilism. After
P, Melville's search for truth through his artist-heroes is reduced
to a clever "art of concealment." The study concludes with a discussion of the artist as rebel. (DA: 40-1468)

495. Gracy, John Walter. Herman Melville's Conception of Christ in
Clarel. University of Southern Florida, 1979. 303 pages. Order
79-17,101.

Clarel is "a modern examination of Christian faith" in the form of a
fictionalized travelog. Its major themes come together in Melville's
rendition of the Christ story. The deaths of Nehemiah and Mortmain
indicate that God is at best indifferent to and perhaps capricious
with man's destiny; hence, He is the source of ubiquitous evil in the
world. Man counters by imagining an ideal world without death, but
nature and reality shatter this gospel-oriented fantasy. The story
of the historical Christ is, for Clarel, a type of this human situation. That is, like all of us, Christ preached the Ideal, discovered
evil, and suffered the disillusionment of never attaining the ideal.
In finding this kinship with Christ, Clarel achieves redemption, if
not solace or happiness. (DA: 40-852)

496. Hallam, Clifford Barry. The Double as Incomplete Self: Studies in
Poe, Melville, and Conrad. Miami University, 1979. 180 pages. Order
80-1426.

The doppelganger, or double, is more accurately called a manifestation of an "Incomplete Self," for it is a projection of a character's
failure to achieve a psychic integration. "The confessional Double
story" is a first-person, participatory, narrative in which the
speaker engages in three psychological patterns: repression (often
expressed in the murder of the double), denial (a less-drastic but
still guilt-ridden form of rejecting the other), and integration (a
painful but healthy acceptance of the other and thus one's self).
"Bartleby" exhibits the pattern of denial. HM: 87-151. (DA:
40-4026)

497. Hayes, Mary Julia Fuller. "And Warmth and Chill of Wedded Life and
Death": New Hopes and Old Fears in Melville's Later Poetry. Florida
State University, 1979. 251 pages. Order 80-6271.

Melville's rarely-studied late poems (John Marr, Timoleon, Weeds) and
his poetics in general "recognized defeat as an integral part of

ultimate victory." That is, struggle and defeat give rise to pain but also "peace and hope." Although John Marr returns to old Melvillean ground, it lacks the stormy questing and settles for a highly personal (non-traditional) "scheme of faith." In Timoleon, Melville reflects upon the healing powers of art and rejects orthodox Christianity. Weeds demonstrates an immersion in the facts of life, the "cycles and workings of nature," and the bond of love. (DA: 40-5056)

498. Heidman, Mark. Melville and the Bible: Leading Themes in the Marginalia and Major Fiction, 1850-1856. Yale University, 1979. 305 pages. Order 81-21,415.

Melville's markings in three bibles reveal continued interest in the literary aspects of biblical books, wisdom and skepticism, natural theology, a strict divinity, and God's grace. Melville relied more heavily upon the Bible than has been previously surmised. The Book of Job serves as the structural paradigm for MD. Biblical allusions in P are more thematic than structural and tend to recapitulate MD. Like the parables, "Bartleby" reveals the "difficulty of living by grace rather than merit." In CM, the Bible becomes a complex but dependable guide to human nature. (DA: 42-1635)

498.5 Hinds, Carolyn Joyce Myers. A Study of Narrative Tone in the Piazza Tales. Oklahoma State University, 1979. 152 pages. Order 80-3583.

Melville's layered ironies in the tales are best examined through the study of the author's techniques in camouflaging his implied authors. Melville's use of limited narrators, his subversive manipulation of reader expectations, and his diversion of our attention from symbolic content produce a "peculiar tone or texture," a conflict between the author's "desire to communicate and a fear of revealing too much." (DA: 40-4595)

499. Hohlt, David Theodor. The Eagle Tries His Wings: A Study of Philosophical Aspects of Melville's Mardi. Texas A & M University, 1979. 317 pages. Order 80-11,955.

M is an abundant resource for Melville's philosophizing and requires more systematic treatment. Impediments to such a study are the problems of authority (when and through whom does Melville speak for himself) and terminology (Melville was sometimes vague). Despite the mare's nest of narrative voices in M (see Stern), a consistent, omniscient voice appears in four distinct chapters and in various lines throughout the novel. This voice is the authority for Melville's philosophy. The vague terminology must be defined only in context. Separate chapters discuss Melville's metaphysics (theistic but enigmatic), epistemology (dynamic but relativist), and ethics (Christian fraternity). Of the three, the latter is most clearly defined. (DA: 40-6278)

500. Kowalski, Michael Lee. The Perils of Pierre: Melville and the Popular Culture. University of California at Berkeley, 1979. 217 pages. Order 80-14,763.

While Melville may have drawn from Bulwer-Lytton's Zanoni in the composition of P, he was more likely influenced by various character

types (the Byronic hero, the mysterious woman, the dandy) taken from
domestic romances of the day. The novel's narrator uses skepticism
and sentimentalism to undercut the mode of the "easy chair" narrator
prevalent among the scribblers of the 1840's. Furthermore, Melville
subverts conventional thought by adopting it in the novel and watch-
ing it lead to disaster. The Young America section signals Pierre's
transformation from a rural to an urban hero. The study concludes
with a case for the novel's thematic unity and a comparison of the
novel to another similar popular work of the day, Joseph Field's Job
and His Children. (DA: 41-252)

501. Lind, Mary Jane. They Summoned Death to Challenge Dread: The
Function of Parable in the Poetry of Herman Melville, Emily Dickinson and
Their Puritan Antecedents. University of Washington, 1979. 313 pages.
Order 79-17,598.

The parable operates on the assumption that the physical world
contains a spiritual (parabolic) realm that affirms the spirituality
of "those who apprehend it." Both Dickinson and Melville use parabolic language to transcend personal anxiety but without denying
their dread nor their impulse toward spirituality. Both fashion
their parables to be enigmatic, forcing the reader to interpret and
thereby test his spiritual identity. In short, the poems lead the
reader to a crisis of self-identity. Chapters I and II define the
parable and investigate the poets' access to the parable through
their Puritan heritage. As a parable of death, Clarel challenges our
religious assumptions and forces us to see the hero's resurrection as
problematic and that doubt is an integral part of the process of
belief. HM: 127-200. (DA: 40-853)

502. Miner-Quinn, Paula Lois. Pierre's Sexuality: A Psychoanalytic
Interpretation of Herman Melville's Pierre, or, the Ambiguities. University of Toledo, 1979. 53 pages. Order 80-2686.

He's gay. (DA: 40-5057)

See: Miner-Quinn, Paula. "Pierre's Sexuality: A Psycholanalytic
Interpretation of Herman Melville's Pierre, or the Ambiguities,"
University of Hartford Studies in Literature, 13, ii (1981): 111-21.

503. Mitchell, Bruce Eardley. Women and the Male Quester in Herman
Melville's Typee, Mardi, and Pierre. Northwestern University (Education),
1979. 150 pages. Order 79-27,407.

Women are "conduits of knowledge" for the male protagonists in T, M,
and P. They help to define the quester's reality, distinguish for
him truth in both the self and world, and lead him from youth to
maturity. Fayaway shows the duality of the material world. Annatoo,
Hautia, and Yillah expose Taji to capricious bravery, sensuality, and
the ideal. Pierre rejects the "false Eden" of Mrs. Glendinning and
pursues the "evil Hell" of Isabel, "and plunges into a vortex of
'corruption and death.'" (DA: 40-3168)

504. Mowder, William Joseph. Identity in the Early Novels of Herman
Melville. Indiana University, 1979. 193 pages. Order 80-669.

Personal identity derives from a conflict between the will's desire
for perfection and finite experience. The protagonists in each of
Melville's first five novels demonstrate a developmental stage in the
growth of a consciousness. Although Tommo fails to find a resolution
to the conflict, the following heroes adopt new strategies for
reducing "the pain caused by the will's futile striving." Tommo in O
achieves the acceptance of pain that he lacked in T. Media's middle
course between Taji and Babbalanja is an abdication of idealism and
an embracing of humanity. This pattern along with a renunciation of
the past also epitomizes the growth of Redburn and White Jacket.
While the early heroes accept their inability to know absolutes, the
later protagonists are plagued by the problem of knowing anything at
all. (DA: 40-4042)

505. Murray, Charles Joseph. A Concordance to Melville's Billy Budd.
Miami University, 1979. 743 pages. Order 80-13,432.

The Hayford-Sealts edition is the text for this computer assisted
concordance of the 5,821 distinct words used in BB. Seven words (a,
an, and, in, of, the, to) are omitted, but frequencies are supplied
on page xxix of the introduction. The 23,746 entries include a
frequency listing for each word, sizable contexts, references to
chapter, page, and line; and an indication of the speaker of the word
(whether a character or the narrator). Appendices list all words
that appear more than ten times in the order of their frequency
("The" is most frequent, "as" is 12th, "no" is 35th), and the pro-
grams used to generate the concordance. (DA: 40-6282)

506. Peterson, Marvin Venzil. The Open Literary Form of Melville's Mardi
and Moby-Dick. University of Nebraska at Lincoln, 1979. 250 pages.
Order 80-2303.

"Open form is a different open literary form from openness." The
former relates to "stream of consciousness" within a narrative; the
latter, to purposely unresolved conflicts. Both "opennesses" come
together in this study to elucidate M and MD. Essentially, MD
refines the qualities of "open form" and "openness" initiated in M.
(DA: 40-4043)

507. Probert, Kenneth Gordon. Romance by Intent: A Study of Generic
Procedure in The Blithedale Romance, Moby-Dick, The American, and The
Great Gatsby. York University (Canada), 1979.

The Romance is a form of "twice-told, conventional fiction" and
"extended allusion." Like a Medieval narrative romance, MD employs
the "norms and themes of monster slaying and marvellous sea-voyage
romances." (DA: 40-5040)

508. Richardson, William D. The Possibility of Harmony between the
Races: An Inquiry into the Thought of Jefferson, Tocqueville, Lincoln and
Melville. SUNY-Buffalo, 1979. Order 79-13,919.

In their writings, Jefferson, Tocqueville, and Lincoln address
America's race problem in terms of its nature and resolution. Added
to this is Melville, whose "Benito Cereno" speaks to two audiences:
one conservative, the other liberal. Intending to educate both,

Melville fashions different arguments for each. From the conservative, white, middle-class "citizen perspective," Delano is the hero
whose American ingenuity prevails over black treachery and racism.
But beneath this is a convert or "statesman perspective" which
suggests that "the clash between black and white is unavoidable."
HM: 161-257. (DA: 38-7502)

509.   Safian, Joanne Marie. Herman Melville and Albert Camus: A Comparative Study. Syracuse University, 1979. 110 pages. Order 79-25,598.

Camus read BB and perhaps MD, P, and "Benito Cereno." While no
direct influence of Melville on the existentialist can be drawn, the
two share similar attitudes toward life and art. Like Melville,
Camus both "protests" and "accepts" reality and denounces romantic
subjectivism and romance fiction. Melville also inspired Camus as a
"painter of the Absurd." Discussions of the works indicate other
areas of Melville's thought, not recorded by Camus, which the existentialist would have found compatible. (DA: 40-2653)

510.   Sarru, Boulos Abdulla. The Tragic Hero in Herman Melville's Fiction. Indiana University, 1979. 196 pages. Order 80-7969.

The early works record the progress of the development of Melville's
tragic hero from Tommo's naive contact with the primitive to Ahab's
mad attempt to circumvent evil. Like Tommo, but in a civilized
context, Redburn and White Jacket search for a better society. In M,
the hero moves from indifference to involvement in ridding the world
of evil. (DA: 40-5444)

511.   Strelow, Michael Herbert. Emerson's Paradigm of the Self and Its
Manifestations in the Work of Melville and Thoreau. University of Oregon,
1979. 242 pages. Order 80-5807.

According to Thomas Kuhn, the history of science develops paradigmat-
ically. One paradigm for the workings of the world suffices until a
sufficient number of anomalous facts emerge which cannot be accounted
for and which lead to the creation of a new paradigm. "Normal
science" is the resolving of problems by the "practitioners" of the
accepted paradigm. With caution, this approach can be applied to
literature. Emerson's notion of the self (as delineated in
"Circles"), fed by American politics and economics and European
science, served as a paradigm which the practitioners, Thoreau and
Melville, applied in their works. Despite its flaws, P is a finer
rendering of material that Melville grossly displayed in MD, for P is
the more effective actualization of Emerson's paradigm of the self.
HM: 67-176. (DA: 40-5444)

512.   Thacker, Victor Larry. Herman Melville and the Art of Leadership.
University of North Carolina at Chapel Hill, 1979. 223 pages. Order
79-25,974.

Melville's reputation as an anti-authoritarian is inaccurately based
upon his strong complaints about the abuse of power in R and WJ.
Throughout the works, he portrays various leaders, but none is able
to achieve the ideal balance of head and heart (intellect/discipline
and inspiration/compassion). The first three novels demonstrate

Melville's awareness of the need for and problems of an ideal leader, and he presents three types of leadership in his captains, kings, and young narrators. R, WJ, and MD give us leaders who lack heart. The closest any of Melville's characters come to the ideal is in the balance struck by John Paul Jones and Vere. (DA: 40-4600)

513. Thompson, Gary Lee. Fictive Models: Carlyle's Sartor Resartus, Melville's The Confidence-Man, Gaddis' The Recognitions, and Pynchon's Gravity's Rainbow. Rice University, 1979. 409 pages. Order 79-19,638.

The four works studied share in common the fact that each presents the reader with a new model of human behavior. Such fictions, then, strive to transform the reader from an old to a new vision. In confronting the confidence man in CM, the reader is forced to make interpretations and realize that "interpretation is necessarily imposed not inherent." The reader's participation in finding the relationship of word to thing, signifier to signified, is in effect a test of his confidence. HM: 71-157. (DA: 40-1462)

514. Treadway, James Lewis. The American Picaresque: 1792-1857. Auburn University, 1979. 137 pages. Order 79-13,691.

As the central figure in the picaresque, the picaro and his nature constitute the essence of the form's approach to the world. More than a simple rogue, this character type demonstrates 1) that ethic which promotes an "immunity to the corrupting forces of the world," 2) a unique relationship to society, and 3) an ambivalent philosophy. While CM does not appear to be picaresque on the surface, it is an extension of the form. Viewed in this manner, the novel's apparent structural problems are understandable. HM: 99-125. (DA: 39-7350)

515. Voloshin, Beverly Rose. The Lockean Tradition in the Gothic Fiction of Brown, Poe, and Melville. University of California at Berkeley, 1979. 277 pages. Order 80-558.

Without a history or established social institutions as resources for literary material, American writers filled the gap by concentrating upon the perceptions of a lone individual. Because the Gothic novel, a form heavily influenced by Locke's representational theory of knowledge, deals primarily with the problem of the perception of appearances, it was readily adaptable to American needs. The gothic is a symbolic method of psychological penetration and of metaphysical quest. Invariably it traces the movement of a character's physical and psychological well-being to a state of peril. The triggering of this shift is nature. The doubting of perception begins in T where the hero is trapped not in a gothic setting but in nature. In MD, the entire world becomes "a perceptual wilderness." HM: 227-261. (DA: 40-4047)

516. Weeks, Charles Andrew. Bartleby's Descendants: The Theme of the White-Collar Worker in Modern Literature. University of Illinois at Champaign, 1979. 311 pages. Order 80-4300.

The theme of the white-collar worker, which begins with "Bartleby," can only be understood in the larger historical (i.e., capitalistic) context from which it arises. Three motives make up the theme. The

worker's occupation is abstract; his class status is ambiguous; and
his personal initiatives at first assert a radical freedom but
ultimately fail to "transcend the objective determinants of existence." With respect to the latter motive, the white-collar worker
may be seen as a Nietzschean figure. The early appearance of this
theme in Melville's tale reveals the paradoxes of "bourgeois or
negative freedom." HM: 73-94. (DA: 40-4584)

517. Wheeler, Isabel Crichlow. Melville's Pierre as a Mannerist Novel.
St. Louis University, 1979. 341 pages. Order 79-23,689.

Mannerism (as discussed by Arnold Hauser) is a 16th century "style of
revolt" in art growing out of the philosophical and intellectual
dilemmas of the Copernican Revolution. It is characterized by
"complexity, ambiguity, provocative literary echoes, wrenched patterns, and mythological depth." Incorporating pastoral and gothic
into the sentimental novel, P is mannerist in its unique structure
and probing of enigmatic profundities. It draws, too, in the mannerist style upon literary precursors and myth. The study concludes
that P's conglomeration or montage of styles and techniques disrupts
classic order in its pursuit of ambiguity and hence it is a "magnif-
icent achievement" in mannerism. (DA: 40-2687)

1980

518. Brucker, Carl William, Jr. The Happy Prisoner: A Study of Melville's Typee and Omoo. Rutgers University, 1980. 309 pages. Order
80-22,545.

Because O is a dialectical outgrowth of T, the two should be seen as
one novel (Typee/Omoo) "which makes a more complete statement than
either does alone." As a "happy prisoner," the narrator of the works
endures dual paradoxes concerning freedom and imprisonments. In T,
he is free but feels suffocated; in O he feels free even when in the
stocks. The narrator in both is also a prisoner of language: his
romantic words in T do not serve him in his experiences and his word
games in O lead him into shallow deceit. Although neither mode
(creative or imitative) is suitable, T/O ends with the hope of an
integration. (DA: 41-1592)

519. Dunbar, Jean Catherine. Words in a Line: Process as Novelistic
Concept and Technique. University of Virginia, 1980. 329 pages. Order
80-22,685.

Language is both static and active. By generating sequences of
language components, the writer creates a process which is itself
"the defining structure of fiction." For Jane Austen, the world
embodies the ideal, and language is a path to that reality. Melville
in the later works, on the other hand, sees a different reality that
requires a different approach to language. Since meaning is not
inherent but contextual, Melville gradually comes to see language as
transaction rather than process. Characterization, therefore,
figures strongly here. Also discussed is Robbe-Grillet. (DA:
41-1574)

520. Georgoudaki, Ekaterini. Melville's Artistic Use of His Journeys to Europe and the Near East. Arizona State University, 1980. 223 pages. Order 81-8071.

Melville borrowed and transformed material from his two journals to heighten various aspects (characters, themes, images, myths) in his fiction. Journal entries helped him shape the sublime features of Ahab and Pierre and provided him images of the decline of the Old World in IP, the tales and CM. Images of wastelands, death, but also transcendence in BP also originate in the journals and reveal Melville's disillusionment with the American dream. The sources for Clarel indicate the author's disenchantment with Palestine's ability to answer his psychological needs. The Journals also reveal a conflict between classical and picturesque aesthetics. Melville ultimately favors the latter and unites it with the sublime in BB to form the myth of the Handsome Sailor, a figure that also appears in the journals. (DA: 41-4400)

521. Gongre, Charles Edward. Unlike Things Must Meet: Metaphor in the Novels of Herman Melville. North Texas State University, 1980. 292 pages. Order 80-21,897.

This statistical analysis of Melville's use of metaphor in his nine principal novels (BB and the tales are not included) groups the 14,000 instances of metaphor into three categories: 1) intellectual, spiritual, emotional life; 2) daily life, and 3) Nature. The ratio of metaphors to pages (the Russell and Russell Standard Edition was used) for each novel reveals a sharp increase in metaphorizing in the later works (T = 1.25; MD = 5.00; P = 5.59); however, ratios for IP (3.91) and CM (4.12) are slightly lower. Twenty-six appendices list statistical data for all categories and sub-categories, as well as for personification. (DA: 41-1595)

522. Kearns, Michael Shannon. Anatomy of the Mind: Mid-Nineteenth Century Psychology and the Works of Nathaniel Hawthorne, Charlotte Bronte, Charles Dickens, and Herman Melville. University of California at Davis, 1980. 376 pages. Order 80-27,063.

An examination of intellectual history suggests that three important fields of the "Establishment Psychology" (or the accepted norms of the "moral science" of the day) are important in the study of British and American authors; they are psychology, Mental health, and Mental growth. Melville's works indicate that psychologically his protagonists move but do not evolve (orthogenesis). While in some cases Melville seems to be an associationist (as in R), he is more generally an "empiricist" depending solely upon the accumulation of data for the attainment of psychological awareness (rather than a rationalist who adheres to innate patterns of thought). HM: 295-344. (DA: 41-2613)

523. Kier, Kathleen E. An Annotated Edition of Melville's White Jacket. Columbia University, 1980. 278 pages. Order 80-16,967.

A densely allusive work, WJ has eluded annotation in America. This edition notes two genres of allusion: references to hierarchy and to the underpinnings of hierarchy. The effect of the image patterns is a serious condemnation of authorities (despite the novel's apparent light-hearted posing of the matter). The annotations further indicate Melville's dependence upon popular, secondary sources rather than primary sources. (DA: 41-673)

524. Meacham, Gloria Horsley. Selected Nineteenth Century Interpretations of Organized Slave Resistance: Black Character and Consciousness as Represented in the Fictional Works of Harriet Beecher Stowe, Herman Melville, and Martin Robinson Delany and Related Historical Sources. Cornell University, 1980. 209 pages. Order 81-2945.

Having relied upon documents which tended to refute racial stereotypes and the notion that slave uprising was merely aberrant behavior, the writers discussed might (one would think) also refute "racialist images." But Melville's "conscious distortions of his factual source" for "Benito Cereno" and his characterization of the demonic Babo suggest that the author belittled the African's struggle for liberation. HM: 79-128. (DA: 41-3583)

525. Meriwether, Mary Stuart. The Fictional Leitmotif in Novels by Melville, Joyce, and Lawrence. University of North Carolina at Chapel Hill, 1980. 235 pages. Order 80-22,488.

Like Wagner's musical use of Leitmotif, the fictional leitmotif is a repeated use of an archetypal symbol associated with a particular character and which reveals inner or concealed meaning. The leitmotif may develop from definition and conflict to resolution, and it may be a vehicle for a theme. Thus, it has structural as well as thematic significance. The leitmotif for MD is fire. It reflects Ahab's character, and its development (in the Quarter Deck, Try Works, Candles, and concluding chapters) adds to the unity of the novel. HM: 22-54. (DA: 41-1587)

526. Raff, Heather Ann. Melville's Aesthetic Strategies. McGill University, 1980. 196 pages.

Melville's works experiment with "ways of seeing" and show that language and culture shape perception. Conversely, modes of perception influence aesthetics. Tensions and movement in T are located in the perceiver's meditations which pass from one mental set to another. In WJ, an innocent views an evil world, but to gain varying perspectives, he must necessarily immerse himself in the world. Thus, there is the peace aloft and the reality below decks. Ishmael endures a "vast detachment" throughout MD, but also a "steady vital entry into centers of experience." While the early fiction gains its power from the development of mediatation, the aesthetics of the subsequent works changes. Recognizing that preconception shapes perception, Melville shifts his attention to self-conscious artistry. The later fiction (P, PT, CM) is, then, characteristically dramatic. (DA: 41-3585)

527. Samson, John William. Melville's Narratives of Facts. Cornell University, 1980. 297 pages. Order 81-2968.

"The literature of exploration" is composed primarily of narratives of facts which pursue four goals: scientific, religious, commercial,

and millenial. Melville researched such narratives, modified their
facts with his own perceptions, and presented them again in his own
narratives of facts. The originals are more than sources; they are
the subjects of his writing. Four works reflect the four goals of
the traditional narrative of facts. Tommo's experiences run counter
to his preconceived racism and argue for cultural relativism, but he
balks at the alternatives. Sacred and profane worlds collide in O.
Romanticized narratives of facts mislead Redburn in a world of
commerce. Both an elitist and millenialist, White Jacket chooses to
await a new political era rather than effect present-day reform.
(DA: 41-3586)

528. Sheldon, Leslie Elmer. The Illimitable Ocean: Herman Melville's
Artistic Response to Paradise Lost in Moby-Dick, Typee, and Billy Budd.
University of Toronto, 1980.

MD, T, and BB (discussed in that order to emphasize the lack of
thematic progression in Melville's allusions) reveal a deeper debt to
Milton than previously surmised. Going beyond mere verbal links, the
study focuses on parallels to Paradise Lost's characterization (Ahab
and Lucifer), confrontations (Eden and its loss), and conception of
nature. In short, the epic poem is "a repository of myth and art"
into which Melville freely dipped. (DA: 41-2608)

See: Sheldon, Leslie E. "'That Anaconda of an Old Man' and Milton's
Satan." Melville Society Extracts. 26: 11. "Melville's Billy
Budd," Explicator, 38, ii: 44-46.

529. Timmons, Theresa Cullen. Herman Melville: The Metaphor of Narcissus. University of Georgia, 1980. 209 pages. Order 80-23,181.

Narcissism is the projection of the self into the world and the
fruitless attempt to grasp that image. It is also a key factor in
the works through P. This study discusses these works in terms of
three phases of the metaphor (vision, phantoms, and diving). The
image pattern elucidates Melville's epistemology and gives unity to
works which appear to be "botches." (DA: 41-1601)

530. Tsomondo, Thorell A. Porter. Literature as Fictional Theory:
Studies in Selected Works of Shakespeare, Melville and Keats. SUNY-
Buffalo, 1980. 149 pages. Order 80-27,640.

Fiction is a process of naming which in turn generates various mental
transformations in the reader. It is, therefore, an "action" in the
sense that it effects changes in the reader and requires of him a
response or reaction (either an alteration or a re-alignment). Thus,
MD with its shifting focus and continually reconstructed perceptions,
engages the reader in a "performance." CM, in all its complexity, is
"a magnified specimen of fictional contrivance" that then acts to
"magnify the problems it seeks to elucidate." (DA: 41-2622)

530.5 Wenke, John Paul. Freedom in Fiction of Herman Melville.
University of Connecticut, 1980. 280 pages. Order 81-6703.

In the tradition of American millenialism (from Edwards to Emerson),
Melville's fictive exploration of the conflict between freedom and

necessity defines his understanding of identity. Ishmael is the
culmination of earlier heroes, for he strikes a balance between
"unimpeded assertions of will and total subjugation" to external
forces. Absolutists such as Taji, Ahab, and Pierre fail to recognize
the possibility of ambiguity. The confidence man's "totalitarianism"
suggests Melville's increasing bitterness over the fate of human
possibility. Throughout the works, the sea is an image of freedom
bounded by the land (necessity). (DA: 41-4037)

530.8 Yoder, John Durbin. Melville, Manifest Destiny, and American
Mission in the 1840's. University of Iowa, 1980. 451 pages. Order
81-14,320.

Melville's seemingly ambivalent attitude toward America in the 1840's
can be resolved through an understanding of the author's brand of
nationalism (a form typical among his contemporaries). While he saw
America as an ideal model for a democratic republic, he despised
conquest. A nationalist but not an expansionist, he attacks those
who assume America's political and cultural superiority but affirms
the nation's potential as a leader of nations. Melville's fiction
from T to CM is critical of Western ethnocentrism. Ahab, for
instance, dramatizes America's "selfishness and savagery."
(DA: 42-218)

Addendum

Since this edition went to press, two 1980 dissertations have come to light. Because of time restraints, these items have not been annotated or indexed. They are

521.5 Karcher, Carolyn Lury. *Shadow Over the Promised Land: Slavery, Race, and Violence in Melville's America*. University of Maryland, 1980. 519 pages. Order 81-1649. *DA*: 42-703.

    See: Karcher, Carolyn. *Shadow Over the Promised Land*. Louisiana State University Press, 1980.

522.5 Kenny, Rosemary Austin. *Melville's Short Fiction: A Methodology of Unknowing*. University of Wisconsin-Madison, 1980. 381 pages. Order 81-11,466. *DA*: 42-703.

Appendices

Possible Melville
Dissertations

531. Hunt, Theodore. *Le roman américain, 1830–1850*. University of Paris, 1937. (*DEAL*, 1864)

Melville in the Graduate Schools

1924–1950
total theses = 37
institutions = 17 (4 foreign)

1. Yale (12)
2. Chicago (5)
3. Chapel Hill (3)
4. Harvard, Princeton,
   University of Washington (2)
5. Eleven schools (1), including:
   Michigan
   Minnesota
   Columbia

1951–1960
total theses = 57
institutions = 37 (8 foreign)

1. Wisconsin (6)
2. Stanford, Vanderbilt,
   Yale (3)
3. Eight schools (2), including:
   Harvard
   Indiana
   Northwestern
   New York University
   Ohio State
4. Twenty-six schools (1), including:
   Chicago
   Columbia
   Duke

1961–1970
total theses = 146
institutions = 62 (14 foreign)

1. Northwestern (10)
2. Columbia (9)
3. New York University (8)
4. Duke, Minnesota, Wisconsin (6)
5. UCLA, Tulane (5)
6. Cornell, Illinois, Indiana (4)
7. Six schools (3), including:
   Chapel Hill
   Harvard
   Yale
8. Sixteen schools (2), including:
   Chicago
9. Twenty-nine schools (1)

1971–1980
total theses = 291
institutions = 108 (14 foreign)

1. Indiana, Yale (11)
2. SUNY-Buffalo (10)
3. Duke, Ohio State (8)
4. Pennsylvania (7)
5. Cornell, Michigan (6)
6. UC-Berkeley, Rugers, CUNY
    Tennessee, Minnesota, Wisconsin,
    Chicago (5)
7. Nine schools (4), including:
        Chapel Hill
        Princeton
        Kent State (Ohio)
8. Twenty-one schools (3), including,
        Harvard
        Northwestern
9. Twenty-six schools (2)
10. Thirty-six schools (1)

1924–1980
total theses = 531
institutions = 139 (33 foreign)

1. Yale (29)
2. Indiana
    Wisconsin (17)
3. Duke
    Northwestern (15)
4. Chicago
    Columbia
    Minnesota (13)
5. New York University
    SUNY-Buffalo (12)
6. Cornell
    Harvard
    Chapel Hill
    Ohio State
    Pennsylvania
    Stanford (10)
7. Michigan (9)
8. Vanderbilt (8)

Indices

Author Index

Index of Colleges
and Universities

Subject Index

Skepticism, 45, 163, 168, 227, 281, 379, 400, 414, 422, 453. <u>See also</u>
    Democratic Skepticism, Doubt, Uncertainty
<u>Sketch Book, The</u> (Irving), 457
Slave Resistance, 524
Slavery, 37, 86, 158
Smoking, 357
Social Darwinism, 219
Social Masquerade, 396
Social Stigma, 326
Society, 341, 370
Socrates, 18
Soldier of Fortune, 107
Solipsism, 196
<u>Somers</u> Incident, 57
Sophocles, 294
Sources, HM's use of, 523; for <u>BB</u>, 70; for <u>MD</u>, 20
South Sea, 7, 8, 12, 150, 193
<u>Sometimes a Great Notion</u> (Kesey), 468
Soviet Translation, 269
Space, 291, 413
Spenser, Edmund, 313, 415, 477
Spinoza, Benedict de, 386
Spiritual Crisis, in <u>Clarel</u>, 78
Spiritualism, 179
Sports, 238
Starbuck, 406
Sterne, Laurence, 246, 429
Stowe, Harriet Beecher, 524
Structuralism, 476
Style, 11, 61, 136, 140, 169, 226, 255, 273, 323, 352. <u>See also</u> Ratio
    (linguistic)
Sublime, 291
Success, 304
Survival, 229
Survivor, 224
Symbolic Mode, 336
Symbolic Novel, 107
Symbolic Romance, 157
Symbolism, 6, 30, 31, 32, 113, 116; Christian, 164; circular, 320; color,
    44; geo-cultural, 473; gothic, 160; greenness, 253; in <u>Clarel</u>, 187;
    light and dark, 137; name, 252; sea, 265; time, 320; in <u>T</u> and <u>O</u>, 344.
    <u>See also</u> Imagery
Symbolist Novel, 386
<u>Symposium</u> (Plato), 281
Synonymy, 323

<u>TTT</u> Taji, 291, 438
Tales. <u>See</u> Short Fiction
Tawney, R. H., 349
Taylor, Zachary, HM's articles on, 9
Technology, 117, 293. <u>See also</u> Progress
Teleology, 217
<u>Tempest, The</u>, 376
<u>Tess of the Durbervilles</u> (Hardy), 275
Thackeray, William, 280, 413
Theatre of 1840's, 162

Theatrical Forms, 427
Theatrical Mask, 148
Theology, 122, 202, 380. <u>See also</u> Religion, Religious Thought
Thoreau, Henry David, 23, 79, 125, 485, 511
Thought, 10, 303; early, 17; later, 16; traditional, 90
Tieck, Johann Ludwig, 188
Time, 94, 320; mythical, 244
<u>Timoleon</u>, 72, 88, 92, 497
Timonism, 218
Titanism, 41, 139
Tocqueville, Alexis de, 508
Tommo, 309
Totalitarianism, 392
Tourgée, Albion W., 48
"Town-Ho's Story, The," 46, 232, 318
Tragedy, 129, 251, 372, 510; Promethean, 53. <u>See also</u> Elizabethan Tragedy
Tragic Hero, 124, 287
Tragic Vision, 122, 178, 287
Tragicomedy, 375
Transcendence, 403
Transcendental Hero, 339
Transcendental meditation, 326
Transcendentalism, 112, 146, 329. <u>See also</u> Emerson, Thoreau
Transformational grammar. <u>See</u> Grammar
Translations, Soviet, 269
<u>Travailleurs de la Mer</u> (Hugo), 185
Travel literature, 42, 55, 256, 277
Trilling, Lionel, 233
<u>Tristram Shandy</u> (Sterne), 246
Truth, 385
Turgenev, Ivan, 270
Twain, Mark, 77, 117, 315, 365, 384, 438, 447, 457, 473
<u>Typee, or A Peep at Polynesian Life</u>, 35, 46, 74, 122, 142, 156, 169, 188, 226, 253, 260, 277, 294, 298, 301, 344, 352, 382, 387, 390, 398, 409, 410, 417, 449, 451, 462, 463, 469, 477, 491, 503, 510, 515, 518, 527, 528

<u>UUU</u>
Uncertainty, 475
Understanding, 248
Unamuno, Miguel de, 204
Unitarianism, 202, 415
Updike, John, 243
Ustinov, Peter, 233
Utopianism, 460. <u>See also</u> Ideal Society

<u>VVV</u>
<u>Vanity Fair</u> (Thackeray), 413
Vere, 239, 331, 492, 512
Versification, 177; in <u>Clarel</u>, 259. <u>See also</u> Style
"Verwandlung, Die," 483
Vine, 273
Visual Arts, 131
Vitality, 417
Vocabulary, 323
Voice, 285; cynical, 371

About the Editor

JOHN BRYANT is Assistant Professor of English at the Shenango Valley Campus of Pennsylvania State University. His articles and reviews have appeared in *American Literature, Melville Society Extracts, Modern Language Studies,* and *Journal of the Early Republic.* He is currently editing *A Companion to Melville Studies* for Greenwood Press.

www.ingramcontent.com/pod-product-compliance
Lightning Source LLC
Chambersburg PA
CBHW070444100426
42812CB00004B/1199